Turning Your Passion into Profit

How to Make Money Selling Your Sewing and Crafts

Published by Classic Press USA
7700 Irvine Center Drive, Suite 800
Irvine, California 92618
www.ClassicPressUSA.com

Copyright © Classic Press USA, 2007

Editor: Nigel Blackwell
Proofreading: Professional Pedants, Ltd.

Distributed by Classic Press USA
Proudly printed and bound in the United States

ISBN 978-0-9787127-1-6

Preface

I wrote this book because I wanted to pass on my knowledge. I wanted to share with others how I have started my own company. During the course of my business I have established a successful Internet store, represent a sewing machine manufacturer, published a series of books, appeared on the BBC television show "While You Were Out™," and taught classes at trade shows and conventions. People were always asking me how I did all these things.

I used to have *one* answer to this—I asked. But, I know it isn't as easy as that. To start a business takes energy and guts. It is easy to dream of owning a shop and spending your day creating wonderful products to fill it with. The reality is, however, you won't have time to do much more than just run the store. So, work smart. Don't spend your time in a retail store as a clerk, get out there and make your vision happen. Sell at a trade show once or twice a year. Speak at a convention. Teach a class. Do some or all of these. Give them a try and see what you like. Whatever you want to do, you *can* do it.

I also included some of the mistakes I've made. It isn't always going to be a bed of roses—there will be thorns as well along the way. I've included some of my stories of tough times so that you can learn from my mistakes, and perhaps, not make them yourself.

As you read through this book, remember, you *can* make it happen.

You don't have to just *dream* of success.
   You can turn *your* dreams into reality.
      You *can* **turn your passion into profit.**

Send me a note through the publisher and let me know how you do. I'd love to write a book of your success stories.

Tandi

The Road from Passion to Profit

Passion

Why this Book?..5

How Will this Book Help Me?....................................7

Is it Art or is it Craft?...10

Where's the Accounting Information?............................11

The "Business" of Your Business................................12

A Word on Attitude..14

Worksheet One-Attitude..16

How Did You Answer?..18

Product

What is Your Product?..29

Worksheet Two-Product..30

How Did You Answer?..32

Part of Your New Job is Selling................................40

Sample Call Sheet:..41

Let's Talk about Copyright......................................42

Focus..44

Packaging

How Do I Package My Product?..................................47

Worksheet Three-Packaging....................................51

How do I Package Myself and my Company?......................52

Packaging vs. Merchandising....................................57

Over-Packaging...58

Pricing

How Do I Price My Product?....................................61

Worksheet Four-Pricing..62

My Price is Too High!..66

Wholesale vs. Retail Pricing....................................69

Paying State Taxes...71

Promotion

Promoting Your Product...75
Getting a "Name"..79
Writing a Book and Getting It Published.................................82
Direct Mail Advertising...85
Print Advertising..87
What about TV and Radio?..90
Promote Yourself and Get Paid..91
Promoting Through the Internet...92
Labeling as Promotion..94

Placement

What is Placement?...99
Distribution Channel: Retail Stores......................................100
Distribution Channel: Trade Shows and Conventions.............103
Distribution Channel: Craft Malls...106
Distribution Channel: The Internet.......................................108

Planning

Planning for Your Future...113
Worksheet Five—Before You Start.....................................114
Contact Sheet..116
Worksheet Six—The First Year..117
Worksheet Seven—The Five-Year Plan...............................118

Profit

The Most Important "P"...121
What if I Can't Keep Up with the Work?................................121
Raise Your Prices...121
Streamlining Your Processes..122
The Importance of Profit..122
Now What?..123

Passion

product
packaging
pricing
promotion
placement
planning
profit

Passion

What is it you love to do most? Do you love to sew? Perhaps you spend all your free time making jewelry? You may be a soap maker. Whatever you do, do you love doing it? If so, *that* is your *passion*.

This chapter is about *your* passion. It will discuss the following topics:

- ❖ Why this Book?
- ❖ How Will this Book Help Me?
- ❖ Is it Art or is it Craft?
- ❖ Where's the Accounting Information?
- ❖ The "Business" of Starting Your Business
- ❖ A Word on Attitude
- ❖ *Worksheet One* - Attitude

Why this Book?

This book is about turning your *passion* into *profit*. The dictionary defines passion as, "a strong or extravagant fondness, enthusiasm, or desire for anything." But, what does this mean to you? You have enthusiasm for sewing, quilting, jewelry making, soap making, or any other craft. You have a *passion* for your art. This book is designed to take you from merely creating your crafts to making a profit selling them.

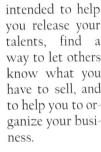

We can have jobs that we work at, day-in and day-out, or we can have a career that we are passionate about.

Think of someone you admire. They have passion about what they do. They truly enjoy their work. Which would you prefer? Working for someone else doing a job or working for yourself doing what *you* love each day? The answer may seem simple; the career that you are passionate about is what you want to do. However, getting there will take a little effort on your part.

This book was designed for you, the one who wants to be selling the beautiful items you make. You are the only one who can make what you make. You are unique. The items you craft are unique. You have a lot of valuable information and talent inside just waiting to burst free. This book is intended to help you release your talents, find a way to let others know what you have to sell, and to help you to organize your business.

Congratulations on your pursuit of your new career. You probably already know much of what you need to do to reach your goals. Use this book as a map to take you on your journey from novice to professional artist.

Throughout this book, you will see old-fashioned pictures of women. They may be sewing, crafting or just relaxing. They are meant to be reminders that women have been creating arts and crafts for a long, long time.

The book contains worksheets and a wealth of tips to help you to learn how to sell what you make. Each section of the book gives the information you need to turn the next corner in your journey to your new future.

This book's tone is that of a very personal discussion from me to you. Hopefully, you will relate to the concepts that are being discussed just as if we were chatting over coffee like old friends.

How Will this Book Help Me?

Everyone who is just starting out always asks similar questions:

> Why would anyone ever buy what I make?
> How do I price my goods?
> How do I get my items in stores?
> Why would anyone purchase from me?
> How do I package my product?
> How do I change my image from amateur to professional?

This book has been written to answer these questions and many, many more.

In Marketing there is a concept called "**The Four Ps.**" These are **Product**, **Pricing**, **Promotion** and **Placement**. This book will expand on this concept so you'll have the answers to the questions you have about how to get started and how to maintain your new business and career.

The "Four Ps" will be covered in this book, not in a sterile academic way, but in a friendly informative way that will make sense to you. Marketing will be covered as it relates to *your* products and services; in a practical manner using examples from the needlework and arts and crafts world.

Now, let's discuss the importance of each of the "Four Ps" as they relate to the sewing and crafting business.

Product

The first of the "Four Ps" is *product*. By now, most of you have probably already decided on your product and that's good. If you haven't yet chosen a product, then through the use of this book and the worksheets you'll be able to focus on what you'd like to create.

This book will also cover ways to make your product unique and special through packaging. Although packaging is not specifically one of the classic "Four Ps" it can make a *huge* difference in your ability to sell your product. Packaging goes beyond your product. It also includes packaging your company and the look you project to the public.

Pricing

Deciding on your product *pricing*—the second of the "Four Ps,"—is always a big question. Will the price be so high that customers won't purchase? Will the price be too low so that it sells well but you can't make a profit?

Pricing is also the area where those new to selling their product often make the biggest mistake. They sell their products and services for much less than they should.

The pricing worksheet will help you to price your products properly so you cover your costs *and* make money. That way you will get paid what you are worth. There will also be a discussion about the various components that go into the pricing decision. All of this will help you maximize your profits, while still keeping your product price attractive to the buyer.

Promotion

The section on *promotion*—the third of the "Four Ps,"—will cover the ways to promote your product through advertising, your web presence, brochures, business cards and more. Promotion is *critical* to sales. If no-one knows about your product, the chances are, unless you are very lucky, you won't sell a thing. You *have* to promote what you do every chance you get.

Placement

The last of the "Four Ps," but equally important, is *placement*. Placement and distribution go hand in hand. This is how you get your product to the customer.

Why Are the "Four Ps" Meaningful?

As you can see, the "Four Ps" are all inter-related. Understanding them will help you become more successful. They will be discussed in a way that will relate to what *you* are going to sell.

As powerful as these marketing concepts are, there is much, much more to this book than just marketing advice. You'll need practical information that pertains to you. You'll need to know about presenting yourself to others in a competent manner. You may want information about attending trade shows and/or selling products at craft malls. You may want to know about getting published and more. *Whatever* you want to know— it's all in here.

Additional Keys to Success: Four More "Ps"

If you can't make a profit, then you just have a hobby.

You have already seen that another "P" was added to the list: **Passion**. Without passion for what you do, it's just a job. You already have that passion and now want to make a living doing what you love. Discussions of the "Four Ps" will help you learn how to channel that passion.

The second key "P" that has been added is *Packaging*. Packaging is generally considered part of Product in the "Four Ps" but it is worthy of being discussed separately in this book.

Another "P" that will be added to the mix is *Planning*. You need to create a plan of action for your business. A plan will help you to define and reach your goals. Think of it as the roadmap to your success.

The final "P," *Profit*, will be discussed last. Without profit, nothing else matters. If you can't make a profit, **then you just have a hobby.**

Is it Art or is it Craft?

It may be a cliché but, Art *is* in the eye of the beholder.

This is a question that has been asked for centuries. Is a handmade basket or quilt Art or Craft? Some people feel that if it's purely decorative, it's Art but, if it's something that can be used then it's Craft. Using this definition, is everything that is merely decorative: Art? Is everything that can be used: Craft? Not always.

It may be a cliché but, Art *is* in the eye of the beholder. Some people call a large canvas painted red—nothing else, just red—Art. These same people may say that an intricately detailed mosaic tabletop is Craft. Does it matter? Not really.

There are plenty of people looking for hand-crafted items that are different from the "cookie cutter" products sold in many stores. Whether they call these hand-crafted items "Art" or "Craft" is irrelevant. How *well* something is made is what makes the difference. What it *looks like* in their home or how it makes them *feel* is what makes the item valuable to a customer, not whether it is Art or Craft.

Where's the
Accounting Information?

There are literally hundreds of books that tell you how to set up your business for tax and accounting reasons. Many books that are supposedly about how to make money in the craft business really only tell you how to set up your accounting. *This* book is devoted to many of the other areas of business.

There are so many sources for setting up the accounting side of your business. First of all, there are numerous inexpensive computer programs that you can purchase that will help you with your accounting. You can also contact your local SCORE office. SCORE, the Service Corps of Retired Executives, is an alliance of volunteer business people who help others start a business. Visit *www.score.org* for forms, templates, business plans and much more information. Lastly, your local library has literally hundreds of books on the subject of setting up accounting and tax records for a beginning business.

Our time here will be spent covering marketing, product, pricing, promotion, placement and other subjects to help you become successful and most importantly, profitable.

After all, if you aren't profitable, then you don't need accounting.

The "Business" of Your Business

Now that you want to start a business you need to build a "real" company. There are several things that a business must have in order to work. Use your accountant or SCORE advisor to help you. They can be a valuable resource for setting up the parts of your business listed below and more.

Checking Account

Although you can use your own checking account for your new business, it is much better to set up a separate checking account just for your company transactions to simplify your accounting. Your bank will give you a list of things they need to open new account for a small business.

Federal Tax Id & State Resale Number

At some point, you will want to be able to purchase your supplies wholesale to save money. Most companies that sell products wholesale require you to have a Federal Tax Id or State Resale Number in order for you to purchase their products at a wholesale price. Some companies will only require one of these, others will want proof of both.

If you have access to the Internet, you can file for your Federal Tax Id on-line at *www.irs.gov* or you can visit your local IRS office in your county to pick up the forms. You may be able to have them mailed to you if you call the office and request them.

To get a Resale Number you apply for one at your local State Franchise Board either in person or on-line. The procedure varies from state-to-state, so you will need to check with the State Franchise Board in your state to find out what requirements they have and what forms you need to fill out. You can find the office in your phonebook or online.

Fictitious Name

If you are going to name your business anything other than your own name, you will probably be required by your county to file a Fictitious Name Statement. This is a document that must be recorded in the County Registrar's office. Usually you will need to publish a statement in a local newspaper as well. Your local newspaper will help you with this as they publish them all the time.

Business License

Some cities require everyone, even home-based businesses, to apply for a business license. Some also require a yearly fee to be paid in order to get the license. They may require a copy of your Fictitious Name Statement as well; if so they will have instructions for this procedure at the City Hall. Check with your city to make sure you comply with their rules and regulations regarding small business.

A Place to Work

Later in this book the place where you work is covered in detail. As a business, you will probably want someplace in your home set aside for you to do your work. Your advisor will help you with the tax benefits and rules for your workplace.

A Word on Attitude

How do you view yourself in the sewing and crafting marketplace? You must already feel you have something special to offer or you wouldn't be reading this book. Attitude, about yourself, about your product and about your customers is *very* important.

Many years ago, I was sitting with a group of friends at a holiday party. We were all in the computer business, but that wasn't what we were discussing that night. Every one of us was talking about how we would like to do something different with their lives. One of my friends wanted to sell the exquisite greeting cards she made each year during the holidays. Another made whimsical candles and soaps and wanted to start selling them. One friend wanted to become a paid speaker. Yet another friend wanted to start an aromatherapy business. Each of us in turn discussed our "fantasy job."

One of my friends from that party years ago followed her dream and became an accomplished teacher and speaker. What was different between her and some of the others who never followed through? Attitude. She "knew" she could do it and because of her attitude, she was able to take action to achieved her goal. She joined the Toastmasters organization to learn how to speak in public. She took classes to learn how to teach. Finally, she started doing the job she always wanted instead of just making a living at her old one.

I decided that night that I wanted to live the dream as well. I went on to create a web-based business selling my own products, taught classes for sewing machine companies, and independently, both in the US and England, became a seamstress for a TV show, lectured at sewing and crafting conferences and trade shows and became an author. I wanted to do it all and now want to show you how *you too* can do anything you want to.

Don't worry that others are selling similar crafts to yours. There is *plenty* of room for new talent, for new products and for new ideas. There is plenty of opportunity for *you* to enter the field of *your* choice.

> ## Attitude, about yourself, about your product and about your customers is *very* important.

Attitude about your product can be so powerful. Do you believe you have the best product in your field? If you do not answer "yes," think about why. Now is not the time to be modest. You need to feel that your product or service is the best there is. You need to know that you are good at what you do—the best even.

There will be lots of people along the way who will give you all kinds of reasons that you will not succeed. They will tell you your dreams are just fantasy. People who don't *believe* they can make their dreams happen never will. You have to trust in yourself and your special capabilities.

Complete *Worksheet One* on the next page. Fill it out as honestly as possible. Let's discuss each of the answers when you are done.

Worksheet One—Attitude

Answer the following questions as if you are *already* a sewing or crafting expert. Find the answer that is closest to what you truly believe.

☐ 1. How do you describe what you do?
   A. My work
   B. My hobby
   C. Something I do once in a while

☐ 2. Where do you perform your work?
   A. I have a studio in my home
   B. I work from my kitchen/garage
   C. I work in a small area of my bedroom
   D. I work in my cube at a company

☐ 3. When someone asks "What you do?" you say...
   A. I am a (fiber, paper, ...) artist
   B. I am a homemaker - I don't really have a job
   C. I work at _____ company

☐ 4. If your Aunt loves your product and wants one you...
   A. Explain your pricing and charge her for it
   B. Offer her a small *"friends and family"* discount
   C. Offer to give her the product for free

☐ 5. The products you sell are...
   A. The best on the market
   B. Almost as good as everyone else's
   C. In need improvement

6. If you get "trapped" by a customer at a trade show, you...
   A. Listen to what she has to say and engage in conversation because customers can help you
   B. Listen for a moment and then excuse yourself
   C. Excuse yourself immediately—after all talking to customers is a real pain

7. Right now I am...
   A. Earning my living with my craft
   B. Not earning as much money as I would like
   C. Not earning any money at all
   D. I'm not in it for the money

8. When a customer places a special order from you, your payment terms are. . .
   A. Payment in advance
   B. One-half in advance, one-half on delivery
   C. Payment on delivery
   D. I never charge

Passion

How Did You Answer?

If you answered "A" to all of the questions, then you are well on your way. You think of yourself as an artist. You work in your studio, not in your kitchen or garage—even if in reality that is exactly where it is. You know the value of your products and are making good money selling them.

If you *didn't* answer all the questions with "A," don't worry. Beginning right now, start calling yourself an artist. From today forward, you are a professional. You are an artist and you do your work in a studio. Your work is valuable, it is unique and doesn't need to be given away for free.

Don't you feel better already?

Let's discuss each of the questions and their answers individually.

1. How do you describe what you do?

It isn't wrong to have a hobby or something you do once in a while for fun, but if you want to make money with your craft, you need to understand that this is your "work." This doesn't mean drudgery, it simply means that you are serious about what you do. The best job in the world is the one you love doing—the one you can't wait to start in the morning and hate to leave in the evening.

2. Where do you perform your work?

Your answer should be "in your studio." Now, does this mean you have to build a studio if you don't have one? Of course not. A studio can be anywhere. Your studio is where you work.

It doesn't matter if you pull out a sewing machine and work at your kitchen table. During the time you are working, you are working "in your studio." Perhaps you work with jewelry on a lap tray in front of the TV at night. That is still your "studio" while you are working.

> Saying you work in a studio sounds more professional than saying you work on a desk built into the closet or in a corner of your bedroom.

Why is this important? Because it gives you the right mindset while you work. Saying you work in a studio sounds more professional than saying you work on a desk built into the closet or in a corner of your bedroom. As I said before, success is about attitude. When you are working in a studio, you have the right attitude about your work. When you talk to others about working in your studio, their impression of what you do is elevated. They will think of you as an artist, not a hobbyist because, after all, everyone knows that an artist works in a studio. Just like you.

There's a television program on one of the do-it-yourself channels that profiles various crafters around the country. Each of these crafters not only call themselves an artist, they invite the viewer into "their studios." When they show their work area; whether it is a space in their garage or kitchen or a spare bedroom, they call it their studio. Why? A studio is more authoritative. The director of the show knows this and tells the crafter to use the term "studio."

3. When someone asks "What do you do?" you say...

If you sew, then you are a *fiber artist*. Just saying you are a sewer just doesn't sound serious enough. You take a scrap of fabric and manipulate it, change it and turn in into something else. That's artistry! You may be a mixed media artist. This is someone who uses a variety of materials to create their art. If you make hand-made paper then you are a *paper artist*. You may work with metal, clay, beads, paint or any number of things. No matter *what* you create, it takes artistic talent to make it.

One of my artist friends takes bits of paper and cardboard and makes antique-looking dolls from them. It would never occur to her to call herself anything other than an artist and that's how everyone else thinks of her. Even if they don't like her art (which I do by the way), she's an artist to everyone she knows.

4. If your Aunt loves your product and wants one you...

This is always a tough one; after all, she's your Aunt. But, you can end up spending all your time working for free if you're not careful. It is easy to fall into the trap of spending a lot of time doing your work for free for those who flatter you; telling you how great your work is and how much they love it.

This doesn't mean you can't give a relative a gift. After all, a gift you make from your own hand (and heart) is much better, and usually more appreciated, than something you purchase from a store. Just don't spend so much time on your "freebies" that there isn't time to make money.

A few years ago, I made linen handkerchiefs for my niece's wedding party. She had offered to pay me for them, but when I presented them to her I told her they were a gift for her wedding. A friend of my niece then wanted me to make some for *her* daughter's wedding. I gave her my card with my regular price sheet, including up-front payments (always carry this kind of information with you—just in case). She was surprised. She had overheard me saying I wasn't going to charge my niece and expected me to do the same for her or at least deeply discount the price. She told me in no uncertain terms that she thought my prices were too high. I didn't lower my prices, they were fair, I just didn't do any work for this lady.

You are in business. No-one else works for free or at a loss and neither should you. The determining factor should be that if someone asks you to create something for them then they should pay. If *you* decide on your own to give someone a gift for their birthday or as a wedding gift, then of course that is *your* choice. If someone wants you to work for them, they should pay a fair price, perhaps at at small discount for family and friends, but they should pay, none-the-less. After all, they are not expected to do *their* jobs for nothing.

If you find yourself uncomfortable asking for money, consider the following scenario:

Aunt Wilma corners you at a family party and says, "You make such beautiful decorative pillows. I've been looking for months for just the right pillows for my new living room couch. I'd just love you to make some for me—then I know they would be perfect."

You're a professional now and professionals get paid.

Would your answer be this?

"Thank you Aunt Wilma. I'd love to. Let's go shopping next week to pick out the fabric. When do you want them done?"

This answer so far doesn't sound wrong. It isn't totally wrong, but it leaves what you will get paid ambiguous. Since you haven't said anything about payment, Aunt Wilma will probably assume that there isn't going to be one. This can end up causing hard feelings either for you, because you don't get paid for your time, or Aunt Wilma, because she didn't expect to pay.

Passion

Don't get stuck working for Aunt Wilma... it doesn't pay!

A better answer would be:

"Thank you Aunt Wilma. I would love to drop by next week with some of my samples. You know I have my own business now. Because you are family I can give you a 20 percent discount over my regular price of $150 per pillow."

You can probably guess by now that the second answer is the way to go. The second answer allows you to be generous to your Aunt without giving away your time and materials. We all like to be flattered, and Aunt Wilma is certainly flattering in her words, but she needs to be flattering in her actions by paying for your time.

The other problem with giving away your time to Aunt Wilma is that it takes time away from being able to create items for customers who are willing to pay in full.

Don't get stuck working for Aunt Wilma... it doesn't pay!

5. The products you sell are...

You should feel that your products are the best on the market. This doesn't mean you have to go around bragging about them all the time—although if you don't tell people how great your products are, no-one else will. However, we are all taught from childhood that bragging is rude. So, you don't have to brag, but you should have the feeling that you have the best product around. At the very least, one of the

Constructive criticism is not a bad thing.

best. How can you expect anyone else to think your products are worthy of purchasing if *you* think they are inferior? Don't be afraid to tell people that your products are superior **and why**.

Now, having said that, they really *should* be the best. If you honestly think they are inadequate then you should re-evaluate your product. What can you do to make them better? Do you need to rethink the embellishment? Perhaps they are not as neat as they need to be? Maybe the colors are not right? Take a good hard look at your products and see how you can enrich them.

If you have a friend or spouse that you can discuss this with, do so. Generally, another person's opinion can be helpful, if for no other reason that it forces you to fully describe and support your decisions. Just the act of explaining something to someone else can help you to focus in on the areas that need improvement and will also help you to see the things that are right. Remember, constructive criticism is *not* a bad thing.

6. If you get "trapped" by a customer at a trade show you...

Customers are the heart and soul of your new business. Because of them you are able to make a living doing what you love. Sometimes when you meet with a customer face-to-face they take a lot of your time. Remember though, without them you would still be working at that desk job.

> Remember, a customer is someone who values your work enough to purchase it.

If you find it uncomfortable to talk to strangers, try to remember that this is someone who values your work enough to purchase it.

Often a customer may want to give you ideas for future work. Listen to them. You may not like the idea they are presenting, but it may inspire you for another product.

Unfortunately, sometimes a customer's comments are not praise, but criticism. This can be especially uncomfortable when speaking with them. Do *not* get angry, but listen and take their opinion as constructively as you can. Most of the time, most people are only trying to help, although there are some people who just want to tell you what is wrong with your product. If they are upset about something that they purchased from you, see what you can do to make it right. Often it doesn't take much to turn a customer from being upset to being happy.

Later when you are alone, evaluate what they said. Accept or reject any part of it that you want.

7. Right now I am...

Right now, you are probably not making much money at your craft. That's why you are reading this book. It is important to remember that one of the many goals you now have, and perhaps the most crucial one, is to make money. How much money depends a lot on you.

Is it possible to make a living in the craft business? You bet it is. There are thousands of people who earn their living selling the crafts they make. More than one industry has started as a "cottage industry" and later became a full-blown corporation. Right now, home-based businesses are booming all over the country. Why not have one of them be yours?

It's okay if currently you are not making as much money as you would like—or even need. Most people starting a new business don't make as much money at first as they want, but if you have a product that people want or need, and you market it properly, you *will* succeed.

Remember, success is one part enthusiasm and one part effort along with a pinch of luck.

8. When a customer places a special order from you, your payment terms are. . .

A special order is one where you are creating something custom for your client. The best position you can be in is to get full payment for your goods prior to starting your work. This gives you the cash to purchase whatever supplies you need. It also means that you don't have to bother with trying to collect payment at the back end.

Getting payment up front isn't as hard as it may seem. People expect to have to pay for goods as they purchase them. If they are paying on your web site, they will need to pay in full prior to checking out of their shopping cart. If you are with them in person, just state simply that it is your policy to receive payment in full.

If you are absolutely uncomfortable with getting full payment up front, at least get one-half with the order. The reason for this is that custom products are not returnable. You generally can't sell these goods to someone else. If the customer changes their mind, you will be out the cost of the supplies and your time.

passion

Product

packaging
pricing
promotion
placement
planning
profit

Product

Webster's definition of a product is:

> "An artifact that has been created by someone or some process or something produced by human or mechanical effort."

Based on this definition, your art certainly is a product. However, as we discussed in the previous chapter, your attitude about every factor of your business will make a big difference to your success. Your attitude about your art needs to be that it is a product that you are selling. This is because you will need to remove yourself from the emotional attachment you have to your art in order to look at it objectively. Understanding that it is ultimately a product will help you to do this.

In this chapter, we will cover the following topics:

- ❖ **What is Your Product?**
- ❖ *Worksheet Two* - **Product**
- ❖ **Part of Your New Job Is Selling**
- ❖ **Sample Call Sheet**
- ❖ **Let's Talk about Copyright**
- ❖ **Focus**

What is Your Product?

Your product is what you sell. Your product is the heart and soul of your business. You probably already have a good idea as to what you want to sell. There are so many products that you can sell. The possibilities are as endless as there are ideas. Think about what you would want to create every day for the next year. Is this what you have always wanted to make? If the answer is "yes," then *that* is your product.

If your answer is "no," that's okay. You have time to work on what your product will be. When choosing a product to produce, start with your interests and abilities. Do you like crafting with wood, fabric, paper, ceramic, or stone? Are you really good at making fountains? Perhaps you make fantastic pillows or Christmas tree skirts. You may enjoy making decorated eggs or stepping stone mosaics? Ideas for products are endless. Look at the things you make for your home, for your family, for gifts. These are probably what you do best.

This chapter is all about your product, how to choose it, its appeal to customers, its uniqueness and more. You will be taken through these subjects one step at a time to help you choose and/or refine what you will be selling. This is because without defining your product and understanding *what* it is that you want to sell, you will have a hard time figuring out how to package it, who you want to sell it to, how much to charge, and so on. This is why *product* is the first of the "Four Ps."

Even if you know *what* you want to sell, you still need to refine and solidify the design. You need to understand what is best about your product and why people will want to purchase it.

Worksheet Two on the next page is about your product. Answer the questions as honestly as you can. Don't worry if you can't answer all the questions; just do the best you can for now. There are no right or wrong answers.

> **You need to understand what is best about your product and why people will want to purchase it.**

Worksheet Two–Product

1. What is your product?

2. Are there other products like yours on the market?

3. What makes *your* product unique or special?

4. Why should the consumer purchase *your* product over others just like it?

5. Are you going to make this yourself or have help?

6. If you are making the product yourself, how much time per day and how many days *every week* do you have to devote to making it?

7. Do you *love* creating your product? Why?

8. What *don't* you like about your product?

9. Is there a demand for what you want to sell?

10. Do you like to talk to people about what you sell?

How Did You Answer?

1. What is your product?

Before you can progress any further you need to know *what* you want to sell. All other decisions you make depend upon this. You can't figure out how your product is unique, decide on packaging, pricing or anything else until you know what you are going to sell.

If you are *still* not sure, put this book aside for a day or two. Do some research. Ask friends and family what they think you do best. You are the only one who can make this crucial decision. After you have decided what your product will be, then continue with this book. Of course, if you want to, you can read the rest of the book and then decide.

Even if you know what you will be selling, talk to your friends and family about it. See what they think. You don't *have* to take what they say as definitive, but do at least consider their opinions. They see your product differently than you do and may have some good suggestions for you.

2. Are there other products like yours on

If you answered "yes," that's okay. There are very few products (unless they are in the field of technology) that you can create that are completely new. Sometimes people think that they have to have a product that no-one else has—only to find out later that the market is flooded with similar goods.

What you sell doesn't have to be new and innovative. It just needs to be presented in a new and innovative way.

It doesn't matter that other people are in the same market as you are. Some of the most well known success stories are about people who "re-invented the wheel." For example, Debbie Fields of Mrs. Fields® made chocolate chip cookies—everyone has a chocolate chip cookie recipe, but she was still wildly successful. Her innovation was that she only sold the cookies for a short amount of time after they came out of the oven.

Martha Stewart marketed homemaking, something that everyone has to do. However, she makes it special, even charming. For her something as mundane as housekeeping has become a billion dollar a year business. Get the idea?

What you sell doesn't have to be new and innovative. It just needs to be presented in a new and innovative way.

How you answer the next question makes the difference between success and failure.

3. What makes *your* product unique or special?

Do you make quilts? What is different about *your* quilts? Perhaps you make baby bibs. Are they prettier than most, more durable or in bright colors? Do you make candles in unusual shapes, colors and scents? Try to look at your product as others do. Look at it as if you are seeing it for first time and are considering purchasing it.

Most likely it is the very reasons that you make your articles that makes them special. What do you add that you have never seen before elsewhere? Did you start making your product as a hobby because you couldn't find it in the stores?

I have a friend who created teddy bears out of antique fabrics and laces. Lots of people before her had made teddy bears. Hers were not only unique in the fabrication, but each bear came with a heart sewn into the toy's chest that had a special saying. She sold these to high-end department stores as a one-of a kind specialty item. They were very expensive and she was very successful selling them.

4. Why should the customer purchase your product?

In this day and age, there are huge discount stores that sell *seemingly* hand-made products for very little money. Sometimes they are hand-made, often even by children or prisoners, in countries where the wages are extremely low. One of the things about your product that can immediately appeal to the consumer is that it is "Proudly Made in the USA." Not everyone wants cheap foreign goods. Quality and patriotism are still highly desirable to many potential buyers.

The articles you sell need to appeal to a particular market. Let's say you are creating soap. Do you make your soaps in a loaf and cut them into bars? These would have a more rustic appeal. Do you use molds and then add artistic decals? If so, your soaps may appeal to a more contemporary market. What is the appeal of your product to the consumer?

Think about the person who will be buying your product. If you are selling fancy children's dresses that Grandma will purchase, then your product will be different from clothes you might make for the girl's mother to buy. Grandma doesn't necessarily look for practical clothing, mother does.

Basically, you need to envision the consumer who will purchase your product and what will appeal to them. Knowing who will purchase your product will help you in designing it. If your product will sell to teenage boys, it will be entirely different than a product designed to sell to grandmothers. Of course, Grandma may purchase a product designed to sell to teenage boys as a gift.

You also need to understand *why* people will buy your product. Try to get inside their minds and figure out what they want or need.

Ask yourself these questions:

- Is your product for everyday use?
- Is it a spontaneous or impulsive purchase?
- Will it be purchased by the person who uses it?
- Will it be bought as a gift for others?
- Is it something that will last forever (durable goods) or be used up immediately (consumable goods)?
- Is your product trendy or traditional?

Answering these questions will help you to formulate the kind of product you are selling. Knowing the answers to the above will also help you with the other "Four Ps." If you know *who* you are selling to, you will price it differently.

Your market will define how you package and promote your product as well. You will market a practical product (that will be used by the person purchasing it) differently from a gift product that you want people to purchase on impulse.

5. Are you going to make this yourself or have help?

If you are going to have help, you'll need to think about whether or not you can train someone else to do what you do. If you can, will they be thorough and take as much care and you would. Also, some products can easily be made en masse by one person. For other products, this would be virtually impossible.

If you need help, can you afford it? You may need to speak with your accountant about how to set up payments for taxes and fees associated with employees. Alternatively, you may be able to hire someone as a *contractor* on a piecework basis. The IRS has rules about this too, so speak with your accountant or SCORE advisor about this.

If possible, it is easiest to keep your employees to yourself and family at first. The laws for paying yourself and family are much more lenient that those for paying other employees. Later when you have more business than you can handle, you can add other employees.

6. If you are making the product yourself, how much time per day do you have to devote to making it?

You need to be realistic about how many units you can make in a month. It is almost impossible to tell what you can produce by making just one or two samples. One of the best ways to estimate how many units you can make a month is to see how many you can make in one day. Take a day or two prior to your test day and gather all the supplies you need for your project. Then spend an entire day making as many as you can. Now you have one day's worth of production.

Figure that it will take you at least 2 days a week for selling, purchasing supplies and administrative work such as filing paperwork, making labels for product, purchasing, packaging, etc. This will give you 3 days devoted to your craft. That means you'll have approximately 12-14 days per month to create your product. Now you can figure out how many you can make without help.

7. Do you *love* creating your product?

This one is pretty obvious. You *have* to love what you do. If not, doing it day-in and day-out will become problematic. The reason for changing careers is to do what you love. If you find after doing this almost every day that you don't love it, you need to find another product.

It's okay if the first product you pick turns out to be too impractical to make, takes too much time to be profitable or is just plain boring to you. You can use the principles you learn in this book for another product. You know the old adage: "If at first you don't succeed, try, try again." This applies here as well. If your first product choice doesn't work, try another, and another.

8. What *don't* you like about your product?

This may be the hardest question for you to answer. Generally, we spend time talking about how great our products are. In this case, the reason for the question is for you to take a very critical look at your products. Is there anything you don't like about them? If so, is this something that can be corrected? Answering these questions forces you to look at your product critically.

9. Is there a demand for what you want to sell?

You may have wondered about this question. How can you tell? How do you know ahead of time if people are willing to pay for your product? Well, the answer is: it's an educated guess. It's a hunch or a feeling you have. There are no guarantees, but there are *some* things you can do to try to predict the salability of your product.

First of all, would *you* buy it? If your answer is "no," there is probably a good chance that no-one else will either. If your answer is "yes," you would buy it, that still isn't enough. You need to do a little research. Have you looked all over for a product like yours and not found one? Is that why you started creating it? Are friends and family always asking you to make one for them? If your answer is "yes." then you have a demand for your product. But family and friends are not the true test of demand.

A good way to find out if there is a demand for your product in the general marketplace, that is among people you *don't* know, is to *test market* your product.

Test Marketing is a way to find out if your product is something that people want to purchase. Create a few samples of your product. Set up appointments with at least ten store managers; one or two is not a large enough sample to give you a realistic picture. See if the buyer likes what you have *enough* to place an order. If they don't then ask why. You may have to rethink or redesign your product to fit the marketplace. If the buyer does like what you have enough to place an order, make some more product and additional sales calls and you are one your way!

10. Do you like to talk to people about what you sell?

This question is a big one! No-one is going to come to you and say, "I hear you make a really great product. I'll order 100." It's possible that someone might hear about your products and ask for details, but you *still* have to follow-up with them. You have to *promote* and *sell* your product. That means you need to enjoy talking to people about what you do. You need to take *every* opportunity you can to promote your product. If you are on an airplane or waiting to be seated at a restaurant then talk to the people around you.

> No-one is going to say, "I hear you make a really great product. I'll order 100." You have to *sell* your product.

It's easy to imagine spending one's day crafting a beautiful product, but you can end up with a whole warehouse full if no-one is buying.

As discussed earlier, the first part is to sell the *appointment*, but then you have to sell the *product*. Once you have the appointment, you need to take a deep breath, put together a few samples of your product and meet with the buyer or the customer at a trade show, store manager or whomever your appointment is with.

Selling is easy for some, but for most of us it isn't. It can be hard to tell someone how great our product or service is when we've been told all of our life that we shouldn't brag. But selling isn't bragging. Go ahead tell them how great your product is. Focus on what makes it unique. Tell them about it. After the first time or two, you'll get the hang of it.

It may take you a few times to figure out what works best for you. This means you may fail a few times. Don't get discouraged: **try, try again.**

Part of Your New Job is Selling

Did you notice that the last two questions in the worksheet were about selling? That's because nothing happens until you sell someone what you have to offer.

Now, this may bring on a sense of panic to many of you. The thought of having to call a gift shop and set up an appointment with the manager or buyer is something you have never done in your life.

If you are at ease in this situation, lucky you. For most of us, this is one of the hardest parts of our new career, but like everything else in life, once you've done it a few times, it becomes effortless.

Naturally, it is easier to do most things if you tackle them one at a time. When you call the store, have a list of questions you that want to ask the store buyer in front of you.

If you have to read them, go ahead and read them, but it's best if you memorize the questions before you call. You may want to practice on friends first to get used to what you are saying. Try to make the words your own. What you say will be more effective if it sounds natural.

One of the things that is helpful to remember is when you contact a store for the first time, you want to sell the *appointment*, **not** your *product*. If you keep your focus on that, it will be easier for you to be successful. After all, you are not selling your product right now, just asking for a few minutes of their time.

On the next page there is a sample call sheet with some questions you may want to have in front of you when you make your calls. These are just samples, feel free to create your own call sheet.

Sample Call Sheet

- May I speak to the buyer for your store?

- Hello, my name is _____ and you are?

- I would like to make an appointment to visit your store and show you my _____ product line that I know your customers will love.

- Is Tuesday morning or Wednesday afternoon better for you?

Take these questions and rephrase them into your own language. It will be much easier for you to memorize them if they are your own words.

If they try to get you to describe your product or start asking a lot of questions about what you are selling, keep selling the appointment. Tell them, "it's best if I show you in person," or a similar phrase. Remember, it is easier for them to say "I'm not interested" over the phone. If you try to sell your product, they may hang up on you before they get a chance to really see what you have to offer. Keep the focus on *getting your foot in the door*.

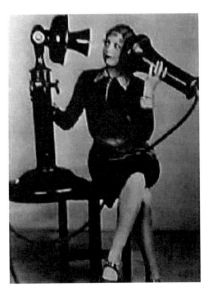

Let's Talk about Copyright ©

Is there a rule of thumb when it comes to using other peoples ideas? Yes. **Don't.** That may sound too simplistic and of course it is. The point here is that you can't use someone else's ideas and/or designs as your own. Having said that, if someone's designs inspire you to create your own design, that is generally okay, as long as the design you used for inspiration and *your* work aren't the same.

What Percentage of "re-use" is Okay?

Is it okay to use a part of someone else's designs or ideas if you only use a small percentage of their design in yours? There are some who say yes. We've all seen the TV shows the day after the Oscars in which they show all the "knock-off" designer dresses that match what the stars were wearing the night before. The people who make these knock-offs often say that if their designs only contain 80 percent or 50 percent of the original design, they aren't copyright infringement. That is more of a rationalization than a truth. You can't take a portion of a person's designs and incorporate it into your own and call it yours. Even if it is legally ok, it is morally wrong. Be safe, and more than that, be honest—don't do it.

What About Using "Licensed" Fabrics?

Can you use licensed fabrics in your products? This one depends. There are some companies, like Disney® and Lucas Films, that say absolutely not! You cannot make product out of fabrics featuring their licensed characters. Other designers and companies are more lenient. If you are not sure, contact the manufacturer and get approval before using licensed fabrics in your products. If you get a letter saying it is okay, keep it forever in a safe place.

Can I Use Commercial Embroidery Designs?

Again, this is up to the designer and/or manufacturer. Many embroidery designers today allow you to use their designs on products you sell as long as you embroider the designs *yourself*. In other words, you can't purchase the designs and have your helpers embroider them. But, even if the designer says "yes." if their embroidery designs are manufactured and distributed by another company, you must get their permission as well.

What about Craft Supplies and Patterns?

Most supplies, as long as they do not contain pictures of licensed images are considered raw materials and are okay to use in your designs. Manufacturers of threads, stabilizers, paints, ceramic tiles, metals, glass, etc. expect that their products will be used to create something else. If you are unsure—ask.

Patterns and kits are a different story. Most of these have a statement on them that they are "intended for home use only" and can't be used to create products to sell. Even if they don't have a statement that they are for home use only, it's not a good idea to use them to create your own products. What you create needs to be uniquely yours. They can't be original and you can't be an artist if all you do is take a kit and sell copies of it or use it to make the finished items to sell. Using someone else's patterns or kits isn't what *this* book is about.

Focus

What does "focus" mean in terms of your product? Focus as we are discussing it here is about remembering what it is you're selling. You should be selling one or two products, not fifteen or twenty. Because you are talented, it is easy to try to set up a business that sells lots and lots of different products. Your handiwork should be part of a coherent "product line," not a group of unrelated goods.

Let's say you sell mosaic stepping stones. It doesn't seem much of a stretch if someone wants you to make them a mosaic table top, and doing so would not be a loss of focus to your product line. However, if someone wanted you to start making them baby blankets, it would be. You may ask, "why not make them a baby blanket if I can do it?" This is a good question, there are many of us who can, and in fact, enjoy creating a lot of different things. The problem is not with your ability to create these diverse products, the problem is that your customers will not know who you are. Do you make mosaics or baby items? You are much better off doing one thing really well. If you go with your strengths, you will become known as "the small company that makes mosaics." When a buyer wants to purchase mosaics, you want them to think of you.

Does this mean that you are stuck making one single item forever? Not at all. You can diversify as long as there is a logical progression. For example, if you make soaps and lotions, you may decide to branch out to gift sets that include hand crafted towels and candles. You may even want to make the fabric covered boxes or hand painted trays that they come in. You are still in the "bath and personal care" market. So adding gift sets to your product line would just be an extension of that.

Even though you can expand and add additional products to your line, at first it is usually best to stick to one or two items until you get a name. Then you can gradually add new products. Keep in mind that some will work and others may not. You will need to test market each new idea, just as you did your first one. That's part of the fun of your new career, you can try new things and have fun at your job.

passion
product

Packaging

pricing
promotion
placement
planning
profit

Packaging

Webster's defines packaging as:

> "The wrapping material around a consumer item that serves to contain, identify, describe, protect, display, promote, and otherwise make the product marketable and keep it clean."

Each element of this definition can apply to your product packaging. Packaging your product properly can set it apart from any similar products in the marketplace.

In this chapter, we will cover the following topics:

- ❖ How Do I Package My Product?
- ❖ *Worksheet Three* - Packaging
- ❖ How Do I Package Myself and My Company?
- ❖ Packaging vs. Merchandising
- ❖ Over-Packaging

How Do I Package My Product?

Packaging a product for sale is an art that some companies spend thousands of dollars on each year. You probably don't have the money or the resources to spend what large corporations do on packaging, but that doesn't mean you can't design the right package for your product—after all, you're an artist.

Packaging is a way for you to make your product unique. It is an effective element in selling your product and it will be covered here extensively. Packaging can sometimes mean the difference between a customer purchasing, or not purchasing of two similarly priced products. Sometimes, packaging is even a reason for choosing a more expensive product. It can make one seem *much* more desirable than the other. Of course, you want *yours* to be the one they choose.

Packaging is also a way of keeping your product clean and tidy. If you will be selling your goods through retail outlets, people will be picking them up and examining them. Packaging will prevent the goods from being soiled.

This chapter will also cover how you present *yourself*—that's packaging as well. When you are meeting with a store buyer, how well you present yourself can make the difference between you being seen as a professional or as an amateur.

The first part of this chapter discusses packaging your products, and the rest of the chapter will talk about packaging you.

Think of your senses when developing your packaging. Try to engage four of the five human senses (sight, sound,

> **Your product is work created by an artist. You want packaging worthy of adding your name to it.**

smell, and touch) to create interest in your product. (The fifth sense, taste isn't often used in packaging!)

Remember, if all else appears the same, engaging the senses in your packaging can make the difference between someone purchasing your product or purchasing someone else's.

Sight

This is the product's appearance. If you are selling candles, do you place them in a decorative box or wrap them in shrink wrap? Do you leave them without any packaging at all? These are the kinds of decisions you need to make. Keep in mind that a candle in a box automatically seems more sophisticated and valuable, and thus more expensive. The same goes for any other product you create.

Another matter to consider is that plain products can be found anywhere. You are creating a "one-of-a-kind boutique" products not "mass produced" items. The packaging of your product should say that with one glance.

You are creating a one-of-a-kind boutique product. The packaging should say that with one glance.

One thing you should always include, if possible, is a *hang tag*. A hang tag is a small label made of card stock that has your logo, your name, your company name, the product's name, size, etc. on the front. Additional information about your product is placed on the back.

A hang tag gives you a chance to tell your story, even to people who are "just browsing." It tells them why *your* product is the best, that it is "Proudly Made in the USA" and how it is different from the others. Your hang tag is a mini "selling pitch" without you being there to talk directly to the customer. Hang tags are discussed in detail on page 94.

Sound

Using the sense of sound can add the feeling of sensuality to your product. When creating towels for sale, I always place a piece of tissue paper inside. When someone picks up the towel, they hear the sound of the tissue paper crinkling. It adds gives a simple towel a feeling of luxury. When making sachets, adding a piece of tracing paper inside gives the same effect. Wrapping your product in cellophane keeps it from being soiled, but the cellophane also adds sound. Adding subtle and delicate sound to your packaging can give your product a marketing edge.

Touch

What does your product feel like when you touch it? If you are selling towels are they soft or crisp to the touch? Either is correct, depending on your preference. A decorative linen towel may be crisp, while a towel to dry crystal may be soft and luxurious. If you sell afghan throws, do they feel soft and squishy, like something you want to snuggle up with on a rainy day? A scratchy terry towel probably won't sell well, while a soft, thick one will.

Touch doesn't always apply just to your product. It can also apply to your package. You may want to box your afghan throws in a smooth lacquered box with a see-though cellophane panel at the top, tied with a silky ribbon. The touch of the package will feed the sense of touch without having to risk finger prints or dirt on the product itself. In the example above, wrapping them in cellophane adds not only sound, but a smooth touch to the product. We tend to like smooth things so this works for many products from candles to sachets, from tiles to ceramic bowls.

Scent

Our sense of smell is very powerful. We can conjure up memories just by smelling certain fragrances. The perfume industry is a billion dollar industry selling scent.

They know just how powerful the sense of smell is!

It may not be appropriate to your product to add scent. However, if you sell candles, soaps or sachets, the consumer will probably want to know what it smells like before they purchase. Next time you are in a bath shop, watch how people pick up products and smell them.

One of the problems with allowing the scent of your products to be open to the air is that it will dissipate after time. One idea is to add the same scent to your packaging. You can brush a little essential oil onto the paper you wrap around your product or onto the hang tag.

Scent is a very personal sense. Something that smells wonderful to one person may be awful to someone else. Keep this in mind if you are creating an unusual scent for your product. Even a wonderful scent can be overdone. We've all had the unfortunate experience of having to sit next to someone wearing too much perfume. Too much of a good thing can put people off. Don't overpower your product with the scent. It should be just a subtle hint.

Neatness

While not a sense, neatness counts. This is almost a cliché, but it is *so* true and applies to your packaging as well as your product. You want your product to sell. If there are drips of glue, (or worse yet, hot glue "strings"), loose decorations, hanging threads or any other things that make your product look sloppy, it won't sell. People will notice work that is not presentable and tidy. Things they *may* overlook when purchasing cheap imported goods, they will *not* overlook when purchasing hand- crafted artwork.

Your product is work created by an artist. You want it to be worthy of adding your name to it.

Keep it Practical

Your packaging has to be practical. I once created packaging for kits to be sold at trade shows that was just beautiful. Each kit was packaged in a small box, suitable to keeping the project in while working on it. It was wrapped in cellophane (that made it sound good when picked up). It was tied with a ribbon and had a nice scented hang tag on it. Everyone loved it. So, what was the problem?

Unfortunately, creating the box for the packaging added about 20 minutes to the time it took to make each kit. It cost an extra two dollars in packaging materials. Because of the competitive cost of kits, I couldn't recoup these costs.

Another problem, and perhaps the worst was that this packing was so bulky that it couldn't be packed in luggage. This increased the cost yet again since the kits had to be shipped to the hotel and stored in the hotel's store room. It took several boxes to ship all of them and the storage costs at the hotel were by the box, not by the weight. Lesson learned. Keep it practical.

Packaging *has* to match the way you are going to sell your product.

As you can see, your packaging has to match the way you are going to sell your product. Packaging doesn't stand alone. Your packaging goes hand-in-hand with your product. As we move on to our other subjects, you'll see how packaging affects your pricing and other areas in your business. Packaging is as much a part of your style as your business card design. Everything you do in your business has an effect on everything else.

Worksheet Three–Packaging

In the space below list ways you can engage each of the senses when you package your product:

Sight

Sound

Touch

Scent

How do I Package Myself *and* My Company?

Package yourself? What's that all about? Why package yourself if you are selling a product? Isn't this just for those that want to teach or lecture? While those who want to teach absolutely should package themselves, they are not the only ones. How you package yourself and your company is extremely important. People will judge you by their first impressions. You often may not get a second chance to impress someone with how good you are. So, make the first impression count. No buyer wants to purchase products from a sloppy looking individual. If your dress is unkept, the assumption will be that you do not pay attention to details in making your product.

Your Personal Image

How you present yourself to the world is significant. How you look gives a non-verbal message to your potential customers about who you are. Over the last decade, our dress code has become more and more informal. What used to be "Casual Friday" in the workplace has now become normal attire for the entire week.

You can put people off by dressing too casually, but you will never err by dressing smartly. Do a little research about the people you are going to go see. For example, if you are going to see the buyer or store owner, go into the store and check out what the sales associates are wearing. If they are all in jeans and tee shirts, you can get away with wearing a nice pair of slacks and a casual jacket. However, if they are all wearing skirts and jackets, you can bet the buyer will expect you to be wearing a suit or skirt and jacket as well. No matter what the staff is wearing, never go on an appointment dressed carelessly. You should look smart and stylish. Make sure your hair and makeup is perfect. You only get *one chance* to make a first impression. That impression can make the difference between them doing business with you or not.

Your Company Image

There is more to presenting yourself than just dressing up for an appointment. You need to present yourself as part of a company—your company. That's right, you are now a professional with a company. You are now an artist-run company. Not only do you have to make a good impression whenever *you* interact with others, *your company* needs to do the same, especially when all someone can see is the company publications and not you.

Also, when you go on an appointment to see someone, you want all the documents and materials you hand them to be as polished as you are.

In this day and age, we often make our first contact through letters or email. Take the time to come up with a complete "look" for your company.

Company Name

Once you choose a name for your company, you are stuck with it, so choose well. Try to choose a name that conveys to everyone what you do. Kountry Korner may seem cute, but it doesn't really tell anyone exactly what you do and some people may think the misspelling looks foolish. Country Kitchen Gadgets may be more descriptive. Additionally, spelling your name in a gimmicky manner may not portray the image you want.

You also want a name that is easy to remember. You also want one that is easy to spell since it will probably be the name of your web site. If the spelling of your name is too unusual then people may not

> There is more to presenting yourself than just dressing up for an appointment.

be able to find you on the web. However, as with all things, there are exceptions. For example, the name of one of my companies is Sew Timeless. People *expect* the spelling to be "sew" instead of "so" because of the industry I'm in. You can do the same if it makes sense to the consumer.

Company Logo and Colors

You don't have to spend a lot of money hiring a graphic artist to create your logo or company colors. There are so many computer programs on the market with stock templates from which you can choose a design for business cards, letterhead, forms and web sites. Most of these programs are under $100 and many under $40. They are as easy to use as any word processing program. Purchase one and let your creativity run free. Use their designs—change the colors and photos to create something that is uniquely you.

Once you have decided on a design, use it for everything you do. Make letterhead, business cards, hang tags for your products all from the same design and using the same logo. This gives you and your business a cohesive look; thus making your company look more polished.

Email Signature Line

It is a good idea to have a standard signature line for your email that includes your web site address and contact information. For example:

> Sincerely,
>
> Kandi Christian
> Sew Timeless
> www.SewTimeless.com
> (800) 555-1212

Change your email program to include this with every email you send. This way, even when you send email to family, friends and business associates, they will see your company information and think of you when they or their friends need products like yours.

Your email address should be professional. It should reflect you and your business. An email name such as Kandi@SewTimeless.com says that you

are in business and also gives the receiver of your email your web site domain name. If you don't have a web site, try using a name such as, JudysJewelry@aol.com. Names like bitzi734@aol.com are not a good choice. Notice the use of capital letters in the email names—not only is it okay to use caps, it helps with the clarity.

Company Tone for Letters and Email

Your writing style should be polished. That's a given. You should take care to use proper grammar and correct spelling. There is no excuse for poor grammar and improper spelling. Take the extra time to proofread everything that you send out—with no exceptions.

If you are creating a brochure, hang tags and other documents, have someone else read them for you. You'll be amazed how

Sew Timeless Logo

many mistakes are sometimes overlooked. Having said that, don't go crazy trying to eliminate every single error. No matter how many times you edit your documents, some errors are bound to slip in. You can always correct errors as you or someone else find them.

Company Style

Is your personal style light, serious, or perky? You should reflect your personality in everything you create for your company. This sets the tone of your company. But, don't try to be something you are not. If your personality is sunny and outgoing, trying to be cool and sophisticated might be hard to do and come off as stuffy. On the other hand, if your personal style is cool and sophisticated, trying to show a company style that is winsome may come off as insincere. When you develop your company style, it should show the world a part of you and should reflect your style and your values.

The pictures you use, your company logo and even the fonts you use are all things that should show your style and personality.

Company Web Site

Most of the Internet companies that offer email services also offer to host your web site as part of their package or for a small additional fee. Use this space to create a web presence. It is no longer optional to have a web site. Use the program discussed earlier for creating your logo and letterhead to create your web pages. Sometimes the company that hosts your site has a program for you to create a web site as well. You only need simple pages that have your company name, logo, your email address, photos and descriptions of your products, a phone number and of course, instructions on how to place an order! Later when you make more sales, you can purchase a shopping cart program or have someone help you create one.

Internet Safety on Your Web Site

In these days of identity theft and other crimes, you *don't* want to have your home address and home telephone or personal cell phone number on your web site and other business materials. For a small fee, you can get a mail box at one of the postal companies. This looks like a real address, rather than a P.O. Box, and there are usually one or two of these companies (like the UPS Store, Postal Annex, or Mail Boxes, etc.) in most cities and towns. For your telephone, there are answering services and on the Internet, there are virtual office companies that answer the phone and forward it to your home phone line. There are also executive suites that will take your mail and answer your phones for a fee. The extra money you spend for these options is worth it for the security you will have for you and your family.

Company résumé

There will come times when someone will want to know more information about your company. This is your company's résumé. It is information about how you started, what your products are, where you are located, and so on.

If you are just starting out, then instead of giving the date your business started, say how long you have been doing your craft. Make it neat and concise and, most of all, professional.

When you print your résumé, print it on heavy-weight paper. This will make it seem more important than if it is printed on standard 20 lb. bond copy paper.

Heavyweight paper will make your résumé see more important than printing it on copy paper.

Your company résumé should also available be in electronic format. It should be in .a standard word processing format (.PDF, .RTF or .DOC) so that it can be emailed as an attachment to anyone who wants to know more about your company. By using these standard formats, the person receiving your résumé will be able to read your attachment.

Since some people are wary of opening attachments because of viruses, be sure to state very clearly in your email that you are attaching a company résumé for them to read.

Packaging vs. Merchandising

Merchandising is different to packaging. Merchandising is how you arrange your products on a shelf, in a window, in a trade show booth or on the walls at a craft mall. You may need to merchandise your products from time to time. Care should be taken to display your products with as much attention to detail as you had when you made them in the first place. Display your products so they tell a story. If you have a variety of colors, you may want to put like colors together. If you are showing a variety of styles, you may want items that highlight the same appearance or materials together. Decorate the area around you. Don't just lay your products out by themselves. Use a table cloth with props, tiny easels, bowls, blocks and so on, to put your products on multiple levels.

After you are done, stand back and try to view your product as if you were a customer looking at them for the first time. Does your display impart the idea you were trying to convey or does it just look like a jumble of disassociated items? If so, rearrange them again until you are happy with the results.

Whether your goods are in a craft mall or a trade show, you will need to keep arranging them again and again as things sell and as consumers pick them up to look at them and don't put them back.

These merchandising displays really show off the beauty of the products.

Over-Packaging

Packaging is important, but over-packaging is a *faux paux*. We've all been the victim of over-packaging. We've all had to struggle to break into those thick plastic surrounds for printer ink or DVDs or had to deal with boxes inside boxes inside boxes. If the packaging draws attention to itself as you open it because it is so excessive, then you need to rethink your packaging. Look at your packaging through the consumer's eyes. Does it seem too much or just right?

Your goods should be packaged well enough to keep them clean and give a good impression, but not so much that people start worrying about the environmental impact of your packaging materials.

passion
product
packaging

Pricing

promotion
placement
planning
profit

Pricing

Pricing is often called the "hardest P" because it is so hard to get right. Price your product too high and no-one will buy it. Price it too low and you cheat yourself. What a dilemma!

In this chapter, we will cover the following topics:

- ❖ How Do I Price My Product?
- ❖ *Worksheet Four*—Pricing
- ❖ My Price is Too High!
- ❖ Wholesale vs. Retail Pricing

How Do I Price My Product?

One of the biggest mistake that novices make is *underpricing* their products. Many times, your friends and relatives expect you to either give your product away or they may expect to just "pay for the materials." Then as your circle of customers grows, you may feel uncomfortable asking for much more money than you did for your friends and relatives. If this sounds like you, repeat again:

"As an artist, I create _____ . I should get paid for my materials *and* my time."

Your art is valuable. Your time is valuable. You use quality materials. You create something unique that can only be purchased from you. You need to get paid for *all* of this. All too often, people just take the cost of their raw materials and double them. This grossly undervalues their goods.

Worksheet Four on the next page, will help you calculate your wholesale costs. There's a little straightforward arithmetic that you'll be walked through one step at a time. Complete one of these worksheets for each product you intend to sell. Once you have filled them out, each worksheet will give you a guideline as to what charge for your products.

The bottom line price that you get from the worksheet is your *wholesale price*. If you are selling *retail* to the public, you should double this price.

Before filling out the worksheet you need to decide how much money you want to make per hour.

Worksheet Four–Pricing

Fill out one of these worksheets for every product you intend to sell.

1	Number of hours required to create one item	
2	Hourly rate of pay you want to make	
3	**Multiply line 1 by line 2**	
4	Raw materials cost, including packaging per item	
5	**Add lines 3 and 4**	
6	Number of items you can make per month	
7	**Multiply line 5 by line 6**	
8	Cost of Advertising per month	
9	Other monthly costs	
10	**Add lines 7, 8 & 9**	
11	**Divide line 10 by line 6** This is your wholesale price **per item**	

Worksheet Four–Example

As you can see from the previous page, you need to decide how much money you want to make per hour. It can be a little tricky.

> ➢ Let's say you want to make soap.
> ➢ Let's also say you want to make $40 per hour.
> ➢ Let's fill out the worksheet for the soap and see what happens.

1	Number of hours required to create one item	.05 hours
2	Hourly rate of pay you want to make	$ 40 / hour
3	**Multiply line 1 by line 2**	$2.00
4	Raw materials cost, including packaging per item	$0.25
5	**Add lines 3 and 4**	$2.25
6	Number of items you can make per month	800
7	**Multiply line 5 by line 6**	$1800.00
8	Cost of Advertising per month	$250.00
9	Other monthly costs	$50.00
10	**Add lines 7, 8 & 9**	$2100.00
11	**Divide line 10 by line 6** This is your wholesale price **per bar**	$2.63

Pricing

From this example, you can see that you should charge around $2.65 per bar. Many people new to the soap business may only charge 50 cents per bar because it cost 25 cents in raw materials. They are grossly underpricing their product. It may sell well, but they won't be able to make a profit because their *real* costs are not covered. Others may only charge $2.25 thinking that this will cover their costs. Charging $2.25 is certainly better than 50 cents, but this doesn't include $300 per month in expenses. During the course of a year, this will heavily cut into their profits.

The wholesale price of $2.65 covers the *complete* costs for creating the product. With this price, you can make the amount of money you want per hour and cover all the costs you have for this product.

Remember, this is the *wholesale* price. The retail price would be around $5.30 per bar. This is a very reasonable price. The market may bear a much higher price. You may find that specialty bath shops sell soap similar to yours for $7.50 a bar. This means you can raise your wholesale price to $3.75 and make more than extra dollar per bar. This money may be used for additional advertising and promotion or it can just be extra money in your pocket.

Calculating Costs

As you can see from the worksheet, it is crucial to include all your costs when determining how much to charge your customers. In our example, if you were to leave out the cost of advertising, you would be losing some of your profit. Yet amortizing these costs over each bar didn't increase the wholesale price to the point where it would be too expensive to make sales.

Keep in mind that the final price you calculate is your wholesale price. This is the price you need to charge your wholesale customers. If you sell to retail customers, the price you calculate should be doubled to give you the retail price.

Shopping as Research - Yeah!

After you calculate your costs, you are not done yet. You need to research the marketplace. In our previous example, the market price for handmade soap was $7.50 per bar. How would you know that? Research. Go shopping. Now you can call shopping research! Look at goods that are similar to yours. Are yours better than those in the marketplace? If so, you can probably get away with charging a little more. Since yours is a high-end product, look in specialty boutiques and stores to make your comparison. Use your best judgement to figure out where *your* product falls in price relative to those already on the market.

My Price is Too High!

hat do you do if the price you calculated on the worksheets is much more than the going rate for similar products on the market? This is why pricing can be tricky. It's a balance between what you want to charge and what the market will bear. This is where your research comes in.

You need to ask yourself the following questions:

1. When you compare your prices to the "market" prices are you making a fair comparison?
2. Is your per-hour rate realistic?
3. Are you purchasing your raw materials retail rather than wholesale?

The answers to these questions have an effect on your pricing. You need to compare your prices with others, taking into consideration the way your product differs from them. You also need to have realistic expectations as to how much money you can get for your product. With a little effort, you can reduce your costs and therefore reduce your prices and still make the kind of money you want to.

Let's review these questions one at a time:

1. What "market" prices are you using?

If you are comparing your prices to one of the big retail giants such as Kmart or Walmart then you are shortchanging yourself. These retail superstores generally purchase inexpensive goods from China or other foreign countries by the container load. *Their* goods are "cheap and cheerful." *Your* goods are made in your country one at a time by you, the artist. The consumer expects yours to cost more. A discerning buyer knows the difference. They will also expect to purchase your goods somewhere other than at a superstore.

Check the prices for similar goods at specialty shops or high-end department stores. Wander through a local art fair and see what items similar to yours sell for. If your prices are *still* too high and your hourly rate and raw materials costs are in order, then you may want to reconsider the product you have chosen, or decide if you can live with less profit per item sold.

2. Are your hourly rates realistic?

If your old job was as Vice President of a company, you probably can't expect to make the same amount of money in the crafts business as you previously did—at least not at first. There are plenty of famous people in this business who make way more than the average Vice President. But if your price is too high, something has to give. It may be more realistic to lower your hourly rate for a while. If that isn't possible, then perhaps you might consider changing your product. Make it more appealing to the upscale marketplace.

3. Are you purchasing your raw materials retail?

If you are still purchasing your supplies at retail stores, that's ok for now. It's a good idea to purchase retail to start off. If you find that you don't like this particular product, or perhaps don't like the business side of crafting at all, then you don't want to end up with a warehouse or garage full of raw materials you can't use in a lifetime.

For the worksheet, lower your costs to the amount they would be if you were to purchase your raw goods wholesale. Generally this will be one-third to one-half of the price you are currently paying.

While you are paying retail, try to use coupons, and purchase during sales to keep your costs down. Once you are sure you are "in the business" for good, start buying wholesale.

When you purchase goods wholesale, although the price is much better than purchasing retail, the downside can be that you must purchase in bulk. The more you buy, the lower the cost per unit. It is a balancing acts to try to purchase enough to get a good price, but not so much that you can't use all the supplies in a month or two.

You will need to contact companies who make the products you want to purchase and ask them what their wholesale policies are. When companies sell to you wholesale, they will have a minimum order amount. This is usually a dollar amount and a unit amount. For example, if you were purchasing linen fabric, they minimum order may be $500. There may also be a minimum order of a full 100 yard bolt for each color of linen ordered. You would have to purchase several 100 yard bolts to reach the $500 minimum.

Purchasing wholesale requires you to have a business license and Federal Tax ID. See page 12 for more information about these.

Even if you are purchasing your raw materials wholesale, take care not to purchase more than you can use in the amount of time it takes to reorder. You don't want to have to rent a warehouse to store your goods—at least not at first.

Wholesale vs. Retail Pricing

uring all this talk about pricing, there were two terms being used: *wholesale* and *retail.* So what exactly do they mean? Each type of customer has it advantages and disadvantages.

Customers Who Purchase Wholesale

Wholesale pricing is the price *you* charge to a customer who is then going to sell your goods to someone else. For example, a retail store will want to purchase from you at *wholesale* pricing and then mark this price up to sell the goods to their *retail* customers.

Be careful when you sell you product at wholesale pricing. Make sure that the buyer is actually a business that sells to the public or stores. It is standard procedure to ask the buyer for a resale licence, a federal tax id and/or copy of their business license. You don't want to sell your product at wholesale prices to someone who claims to be a reseller but isn't.

Wholesalers

There are companies who purchase product from the artist and then sell that product to catalog companies or retail stores. These companies are called wholesalers. They generally want additional discounts, for example 10 percent under wholesale. Be careful with these. Unless you are able to make large amounts of your product, you could be overwhelmed by the size of the order.

However, if you can handle the orders, these companies can be a goldmine.

Generally, you can sell more product by selling your goods wholesale (either directly to the retail stores or to a wholesaler) than you can selling directly to the public. A store or wholesaler will generally place much larger orders than a retail customer would. In fact, you can have a minimum order policy. For example, you can make the minimum order quantity six units or a minimum order of $300 or however you want it. In addition, wholesalers commonly give you repeat business. This helps you. You get additional business without having to find a new customer for each sale.

Retail Customers

If you sell to retail customers, you will price your product about twice as much as if you sell wholesale. At first it may seem to be the best way to go. After all, you make extra profit right? Well, yes and no. You do make *more on each sale* when you sell retail—but, you may sell to

fewer customers who place *smaller* orders, usually one unit at a time. Also, to sell retail may mean that you have additional costs not calculated in the wholesale price. You may have to sell at trade shows, you may need a web site with a shopping cart that takes credit cards which require a transaction fee for each order, you may have to produce a glossy catalog and more. Certainly if you decide to set up a "bricks and mortar" retail store yourself, you will have lots of extra costs, such as rent, utilities and stock on hand. These costs need to be taken into account to ensure your retail price is high enough to cover them and still make you a profit.

Another advantage of selling directly to the end consumer besides the fact that you make more money per unit, is that you get to know your customers individually. Customers you know personally, more likely than not, will refer you to their family and friends. Referrals are the best form of advertising you can have.

Paying State Taxes

If you do sell to retail customers, you will need to collect and pay taxes to your state. To do this, you will need to have a resale license. Page 12 has information about how to obtain one of these or you can ask your accountant or SCORE advisor. Once you collect the money, you will need to file a tax return. The forms for this are available on your state's web site or at their franchise offices.

If you sell to wholesale customers, you will *still* need to do some paperwork if the customer is in your own state. You will need a copy of the customer's resale license to prove that they can purchase goods from you without paying taxes. You will need to fill out tax forms even if you don't have to pay sales tax. There are some States that are insisting that you fill out tax forms even if your customer is not in your state. Again, you may want to discuss this with your accountant or SCORE advisor.

passion
product
packaging
pricing

Promotion

placement
planning
profit

Promotion

All the passion you may have, all the work you put into your product, its pricing and your packaging mean nothing if you don't promote your product.

Promotion involves getting information about your product out to the consumers. People need to know about what you have to offer.

This chapter will cover the following topics:

- ❖ Promoting Your Product
- ❖ Forms of Advertising
- ❖ Getting a "Name"
- ❖ Magazine Articles
- ❖ Writing a Book and Getting it Published
- ❖ Print Advertising
- ❖ What about TV and Radio?
- ❖ Other Ways to Promote Yourself
- ❖ Labeling as Promotion

Promoting Your Product

Never miss an opportunity to talk to someone about your product and hand out your business card. This is probably the most effective way to promote your business. For one thing, it is practically free.

Word of mouth is probably the best form of advertising you can have. If someone recommends you to their friends, chances are you'll make the sale. So, don't be afraid to ask your past customers to tell their friends and family about you. Tell them that if they enjoyed your product and they refer you to someone else then this will help you to stay in business. If you stay in business, they can order from you again. You are good, so they should be happy to tell others about you.

Ways of Advertising

Advertising is essential, but can be expensive. You can spend your entire yearly advertising budget on one advertisement in a national magazine. You may want to do this once you are an established company, but for the first year or two, what do you do?

You will need to find many different ways to advertise without spending too much on a single ad. One alternative, and one that is more focused, is to advertise in a local newsletter. For example, if you are a fiber artist, the American Sewing Guild local chapters each have a newsletter in which you can advertise. These will go to prospective customers in your local area and cost much less than advertising nationally. There may be local clubs for seniors or other community groups that have newsletters. Advertising in these is generally inexpensive and local. It is a good way to start.

There is a whole section later in this book about print advertising. For now, here are some other ways to promote your business.

> You can create excellent cards, flyers, and brochures using a word processing program, glossy paper and an ink jet printer.

Neighborhood Flyers

A one page flyer is an inexpensive way to advertise. Create a one page flyer about your products Make sure it has a picture of your goods, a description and a price. It also must have some way for the consumer to contact you to purchase. These can be posted in neighborhood community centers, on public bulletin boards, and so on.

Business Cards

You should *always* carry your business cards with you at all times. They should contain your logo, company name, your name, your web site address and how to contact you by phone or email. If you print your own business cards from your printer, use glossy stock. There are blank cards available that have no perforations when torn apart and some allow you to print over the edges—giving you a very sophisticated looking card. You can print as few or as many as you need.

Creating a Brochure

A sophisticated looking brochure is an excellent way to promote your business. Full color glossy brochures are very finished looking. But you don't have to spend thousands of dollars having a graphic artist create a brochure for you. You can create an excellent brochure using a word processing program, glossy paper and an ink jet printer. Glossy paper for ink jet printers is available at most stationary or office supply stores. Many of these stores also carry specialty software for creating brochures. These have professionally designed templates for you to use as a basis of your brochure. These programs often have templates for your letterhead, envelopes, business cards as well. This way all your stationary and brochures will match, giving you an even more refined image.

Use every opportunity you can to promote your product.

If you don't have a color ink jet printer, you can purchase "brochure stock" with pre-printed colorful borders that you can print on using any printer. You can also use these in a photocopy machine instead of a printer. This pre-printed stock comes in letterhead, flyers, envelopes, business cards and brochures. Again, this allows you to have a very savvy, cohesive look for very little money.

Once you have your brochures and business cards, call retail store buyers to see if you can stop by to drop off a brochure; anything to get your foot in the door. Buyers are very busy, so do set up an appointment. It is rude to walk in with your goods without an appointment and doing this may backfire on you. Once you are there, give them a brochure and ask if they would like to see your wares. Many times an appointment to drop by a brochure and "meet face-to-face" turns into a full-blown sales call. Always take your products and leave them in the car—just in case.

See if you can place your brochure on the counter of local craft stores, dry cleaners, library bulletin boards and even donut shops. Place them anywhere that the manager will allow.

If you are too far away from the buyer to drop by, mailing a brochure is much more serious than sending an email; though you should send a follow-up email to ensure the buyer received your brochure. Use *every opportunity* you can to contact your prospective customers. If your name is in front of them often, you may have an edge on your competitors. Certainly having an attractive and informative brochure that has a description and picture of your product will help you sell it. Buyers tend to keep brochures and pamphlets in a buying file.

Price Sheets

A price sheet is as necessary as a brochure. It doesn't have to be overly fancy. It can be a simple table showing the product name, a brief description, the unit type (each, pair, dozen, etc.) and the cost to the buyer per unit type, minimum ordering amounts, etc. You can also include a suggested retail price for your product.

The price sheets must be included when you send a brochure. If you visit a buyer in person, give them the price sheet and take the time to explain what you have and how much it will cost them.

The reason for keeping the price sheet separate from your brochure is that your prices generally change more often than your brochure. The brochures cost more to produce than the price sheets. However, you can include your prices in your brochure if you really want to.

Catalogs

A catalog is a combination of your brochure and your price sheet. If you create a catalog, you don't need the other two. You may want to decide if you want your catalog pricing to be wholesale or retail. If it is retail, you will need a separate *wholesale price sheet* as a companion to your catalog. A catalog should have a picture of your product, a full description, the buying unit type and the price per unit.

A catalog only makes sense if you have multiple items or styles to sell. They are also expensive—so only print what you need.

Mailing Lists

Whenever you talk to people, ask them if they want to be on your mailing list.

When people are on your web site, there should be a place for them to sign up to be on your mailing list. You will have two types of mailing lists, physical addresses and email addresses.

Physical Address Lists

These are people who have given you their home or business addresses. There should be a space on your web site for physical addresses as well as email addresses. There will be times that you want the personal touch of a letter, a thank you note, or other such mailing. This list will be used at these times.

Email Address Lists

You will also want to gather email addresses so you can contact your prospect and/or customer base via email. Be careful not to abuse this. We have all been victims of spam (unwanted email). You don't want your customers to feel like you are sending them too much junk email. Also, if a customer requests that you take their name off your email list, do so promptly.

Keep these lists. They are a valuable resource. You can send these people on your list new brochures, changes in pricing and notifications of special sales. This is a great way to increase sales with both your prospects and current customer base.

Getting a "Name"

Self promotion and getting publicity may be one of the harder things you do when you are new to the business. Once you get the hang of it, you'll always be finding opportunities to get your name known.

It can't be over-emphasized that you should "never miss an opportunity to promote your business." Promoting your business also means promoting yourself. Most of us have been taught that it is wrong to promote ourselves so you may feel uncomfortable about this. Remember, this is not vanity, this is *business*.

Talk to your friends and family and let them know what you are doing. Word of mouth is the best form of promotion. Once you start having customers, if they are satisfied, ask them to recommend you to their friends.

If you belong to a church or community group, ask if you can place a promotional display on their bulletin board.

If you are stuck in an airport waiting for a plane or in the dentist office, talk to the person next to you about what you do. Tell them you are an artist. That usually peaks people's interest. Give them your card, or better yet, your brochure and ask them to think of you the next time they are in the market for what you sell.

People have to know who you are. If they remember your name and the name of your company, they can find you in the future when they want to purchase. Always introduce yourself and say the name of your company when you talk to someone you've just met and remind them when you say goodbye.

Trunk Shows

If you feel comfortable enough, hold a "trunk show" at a local craft or fabric store. A trunk show is where you bring samples of your work and talk about them. It is *not* a sales presentation.

Promotion

During your trunk show, you need to talk about the techniques, the historical importance of the art or some other angle. People will be put off if they come to your event and it's just a sales pitch. Your talk needs to be interesting to the audience. Also, give it a catchy title that will intrigue people enough to make them want to attend in the first place.

First design the trunk show. Do some research about your craft and come up with about a one-hour presentation. You can create hand-outs, visual aids, posters, etc. Use your product as part of the presentation.

A trunk show is where you bring samples of your work and talk about them.

Once you have designed your talk, contact local craft and fabric stores. Set up an appointment with the person in charge of classes and presentations—this is usually the store manager. Just like you did when you were calling buyers, just sell the appointment over the phone, not the talk. When you go to the appointment, explain your trunk show, what you will be showing and a little about what you will be explaining to the audience.

Whenever you present a trunk show, your name should be part of the publicity that is sent out by the store manager. When you set up the trunk show, tell the manager that having your name on the store poster, in the newsletter or email that goes out to their customers is a part of your agreement. Having your name in the store publicity is good for both of you. When the materials say "...well known artist..." it adds a sense of authority to the event. This will create excitement about your trunk show. This will get more people to come. That is better for both you and the store.

Also, if you are holding a trunk show, create some inexpensive flyers with your picture on them. Walk around the neighborhood and place them on people's doors. Knock on their door, if they answer, that's an opportunity to talk about what you do. Ask the store manager if you can have your flyers added to the customer's bags as they leave the store with their purchases. If that isn't possible, ask if you can have them in a display on the check-out counter. Provide the store with a clear plastic stand for your flyers. They should be displayed at least 2-3 weeks prior to the event.

Magazine Articles

If you have a unique product, send pictures to magazines. Many magazines are looking for unique products to use in their layouts. These are then listed in their "where to buy" section. Sometimes they even highlight certain products in their "what's new" sections. This is free publicity at its best.

Along with the pictures, you can propose an idea for an article. You can use some of the thoughts from your trunk show presentation to create the article, or you can create a how-to article on how to make something similar to your product. You won't necessarily want to make the exact product. Try coming up with a project that is less complex than the goods you sell. You don't have to write the whole article at this time, just write an outline that makes it very clear what you will be writing for them. Magazines are always looking for well-written articles for their

publication. Yours could be just what they are looking for.

Send your pictures and articles to magazines that target the people you want to sell to. For example if you make bridal gowns, you may want to write an article on how to pick out a gown by body type. You may create a how-to article on how to make a simple veil. These would be sent to bridal magazines. If you make ceramic garden gnomes, then you could write an article showing how to paint pre-made ceramics and send the article to gardening magazines. If you make Christmas tree skirts, you may want to send an article to home decor magazines for their holiday edition. *Get the idea?*

Writing a Book and Getting
It Published

Publishing a book will get you a lot of recognition and respect in your field. You can write a "How-to" book about your craft. Writing a book is not for the faint of heart because getting a book published is probably one of the harder things you will do. Writing a book takes a lot of time and effort. There are rewrites and rewrites and rewrites Also, if you can't take criticism, don't write a book. You should be serious before you embark on book writing. Writing a book will take precious time away from creating your product.

Obtain the services of a good editor and proof-reader—you can't do either of these functions yourself—they will be worth their weight in gold.

There are a lot more budding authors out there than there are publishers. One thing you will want to do is find a publisher who specializes in craft books. They understand the market

you are writing for. They also understand that yours isn't necessarily a million copy seller. Well, it may be, but generally the craft book market is much smaller than other area of the book publishing business.

It may take sending your work to many, many publishers, but if your book is interesting and well written, you have as good of a chance as anyone else of getting it published.

What about self-publishing?

There are lots of people who self-publish. Publishing involves editing, proofreading, printing, binding, distributing, selling and promoting. It is a *big* job. There are lots of books on the subject—most are self-published. It takes great effort to self-publish and *do it well*. Be sure self-publishing is something you want to do.

Take the time to research how to do this *before* embarking on self-publishing.

There is nothing wrong with self-publishing, it is just hard work. If you are well organized and willing to put in the time, you can publish your own book.

You will need to apply for an ISBN (International Standard Book Number) if you want to sell your book to book stores. Take the time to research the international ISBN web site *www.isbninternational.org*. In the United States, you can obtain your ISBN from *www.isbn.org*. By having your own ISBN, *you* will own all rights to your work. Whomever registers the ISBN owns the rights to the book.

If you are going to publish your own book, you will need to find a bookbinder to make the copies. A book that isn't properly bound will look amateurish. I have seen self-published "How-to" books that are spiral bound. They always look like something someone printed in their garage. Is this the image you want for your book? You're going to spend over a year writing and rewriting your book, so spend the money to have it printed and bound by a competent bookbinder.

Vanity Publishers

There are hundreds of companies who are willing to publish your book or any book, for a price. They are called vanity or subsidy publishers. They are not bookbinders, nor are they real publishers. They are very expensive and usually *they* will hold the copyright to your book. Be *very* cautious before giving your book to one of these companies. Many book stores will not accept books published by these companies because they generally print the books as they are submitted; no editing, no proof-reading. They will print *any* book written by *anyone* who is willing to pay their price. You not only pay for the books to be printed at very high prices, but you have to do all the marketing and distribution for your book. The only way you can make money selling your book is if you can sell it at a higher price than the publisher charges you—that is not often possible.

What is POD?

POD stands for "print-on-demand." It is a hybrid of traditional publishing and subsidy printing and originated due to increasing difficulties for authors to be published through traditional methods. The "demand" aspect to this term refers to the fact that rather than print hundreds of copies on a press and physically store the books, digital methods are used to store the books upon completion of editing and typesetting and anywhere from a handful to hundreds of copies are produced "on demand." The costs are generally very high for this service. Be careful with these too. Many vanity presses are now calling themselves PODs.

Traditional Publishers

A "traditional" publisher, on the other hand is one that will review your book prior to accepting it for production and publication. They will then enter into a contract with you, the author. Generally, they own the copyright to your book, at least for the period of time specified in the contract. They will edit and proof-read your book working with you for re-writes. They will pay you royalties on every book sold. Traditional publishers sometimes charge money up front or require that you "work-off" the publishing charges. This means that you do not get any royalties until a established number of books have been sold.

You may have to send your work to several publishers before you find one who is willing to publish your book. Do not take their rejection letters too

personally. They are publishing books to make money. They will only publish yours if they think they can sell enough books to cover all their costs and make a profit.

To find a publisher, check the copyright page of books similar to yours in the bookstore or library. These publishers are used to producing craft books and know that craft books generally do not sell millions of copies.

Independent Publishers

There are publishing companies who are in-between self-publishing and "traditional" publishers. These companies, unlike vanity and POD publishers, will not accept just any book. Often they charge a fee for editing, proof-reading and layout. Once these tasks are accomplished, the book is then printed and distributed to bookstore and retailers at no cost to the author. They pay royalties, just like traditional publishers.

Direct Mail Advertising

A form of advertising your product that can be very effective is direct mail advertising. It is much more expensive that the previously mentioned methods, but if uses properly can give you a good return for your money. Direct marketing involves sending someone a letter and brochure designed to peak their interest and get them to contact you to purchase your goods.

Direct mail is best used to get wholesale customers. For example, if you sell garden statues and signs, you would target gardening shops to send a letter and a brochure. You could look up in the phone book or on the Internet to find all the gardening stores. You could start in your local area and branch out to stores in surrounding areas and so on.

To try to do the same with retail customers would require massive amounts of mail and would be hit-and-miss. There is very little way to know ahead of time if there is anyone in a particular household interested in gardening so, you would have to send to everyone. There are companies who will give some information about certain households, but they are expensive and usually don't have information that is as specific as to whether someone's hobby is gardening or fishing. Finding stores is a much easier task and more appropriate for direct marketing.

Make sure that you direct your letters to the right place. Just as with any form of advertising, in order to be effective, it has to go to the right person. What kind of stores and shops will want to sell your goods? These are the ones you need to send your letters to. Try to get the owner's name so you can direct your letter to them personally.

Store owners and buyers receive marketing letters every day so yours should be simple, short and to the point. Your letter needs to tell them that your product will help their profits. You may want to have a special offer for their first order. State that you have a product that their customers will want to purchase. Tell them how to contact you if they have questions. Enclose a brochure so they have full details. Don't put anything on the outside of the envelope stating things such as "great offer inside" or our mail may never be opened.

Generally, direct marketing letters receive a return of about one to two percent. This means that for every 100 letters you send you can expect to get a response from one or two stores. If you want to up these odds, follow up your letter with a phone call about two weeks after you send it. Remind them of your special offer for their first order and see if they have any question. a follow-up phone call will let the prospective customer know that you are interested in their business.

Don't be surprised if the owner says they never received your letter. That is common. You can always offer to send another brochure. Tell them amount your offer anyway.

Email

Almost everything said about direct mail marketing applies to email marketing. However, never purchase email lists from an outside party. First of all this practice can get your email banned as a spammer (someone who sends unwanted mail). Spamming is now illegal. Secondly and more importantly, the names on the list are probably not worth having. Instead, develop your own list that people "opt-in" to have. Opt-in means that they have to do something to be on your list. There are lots of email processing companies that you can find on the Internet that help you manage your email.

Print Advertising

Print advertising is the most expensive form of promotion. Before you place an ad in a magazine or newspaper, be certain that you place it where it will do the most good.

Do some research. If you make jewelry, you probably won't get many customers by advertising in a magazine focused on people in the jewelry *making* trade. You will be advertising to other jewelry makers just like you. If you make babies quilts, the same holds true. Advertising in a magazine or newsletter for quilters won't make you many sales. These people already know how to quilt so they usually don't purchase them from others. If you make jewelry, you will want to place an ad in a fashion magazine. If you make babies quilts you may want to place ads in a magazine for expectant mothers or one whose demographic is grandmothers. Good ad placement is a big factor in the success of your advertisement.

expenses such as brochures, supplies, letterhead, etc. These will take much of your available money. As discussed earlier, there are other ways to get publicity that don't cost much, if any money. Use these methods first. However, there may come a point when you decide that it is worthwhile to advertise in print. When this time comes, you'll need to proceed with care so you don't spend a lot of money without getting results.

Print Advertising is Expensive

Since print advertising is expensive, you should be able to justify your need for it before you take the plunge. When you first start your business you'll have other

Print Ads Must Look Professional

Companies spend literally millions of dollars each year developing advertising campaigns. When you place an ad in a newspaper or magazine, it must look polished. The ad must grab the readers' attention and initiate action on their part. This doesn't mean you have to pay thousands of dollars to have an ad professionally designed for you. With a good word processing or desktop publishing program you can create your own advertisements. Many of these programs come with templates you can use as a starting point.

Start paying attention to the ads that draw *your* attention. What it is about those ads that you like? What works for you? You can incorporate the ideas you find into your own ads. This doesn't mean you should copy these advertisements—that's copyright infringement; just use them as inspiration to create your own ads.

Before you place the ad, have your friends and family look at it and give their opinion as to whether they think it is effective and looks suitable for your craft. They may not know anymore about ad copy than you do, but another set of eyes may certainly help you look at your ads in a different way.

Newspapers or Magazines?

Once you have your ad copy, you need to decide if you want to place it in a local newspaper, a national newsletter or a national magazine. There are pros and cons to each of these.

National Advertising

National advertising is glamorous. It's exciting to see your ad in full color on the pages of your favorite magazine. Obviously, national magazines give you the most exposure for each ad—but that comes at a price—a high price.

Also, before you decide that you want to advertise nationally, you must be able to handle any business that may result from the ad. If you are selling goods, are you set up to ship nationally? Can you calculate shipping costs easily and quickly? Your shipping costs could go up significantly. Do you charge for the actual shipping amount or a fixed amount for shipping and handling? Can you process orders on your web site, adding shipping and tax when needed? Can you take credit cards? These are questions you must answer "yes" to before you place your advertisement on a national level.

National Newsletters

Newsletters are an alternative to national magazines. Check the Internet for newsletters that cater to the people you want to sell to. They generally charge less for their ad space than the magazines do. You can browse the Internet to find newsletters for just about any area of interest. Try entering "home decor newsletter" or "bridal newsletter" into your search engine and you'll find thousands of them.

Newspapers

Newspapers, on the other hand, reach a local market, at a *much* lower cost. The ads are usually black and white, which makes your cost of developing the ad lower. It is important that the ad bring you enough business, or it will not be a good value. If you have already saturated your local area, it may be time to move to a wider coverage for your ads. Before you take the leap to national ads, you may consider advertising in newspapers in the next city or county.

What about TV and Radio?

Television and radio are even more expensive than national magazines. You've heard all the success stories of people who get their product onto the home shopping channels. If you can make enough of your product to do this, and want to give it a try, go for it. There is no reason to discourage you—others have done this before you and been successful. For most people just starting out, this is a little unrealistic. Production of your product is still on a small scale and unless you have a large start-up budget, your efforts are best used on selling to local stores, on the Internet and so on.

Television Ads

Advertising on television is probably out of the reach of most people with small companies. However, sometimes local cable channels have more reasonable pricing. If you are lucky enough to have a large advertising budget, you may want to explore this. You can reach a lot of people on television. There are companies who, for a fee, will help you create your TV ad.

Radio Ads

Radio is more effective for selling services than it is for products because the customer can't *see* what you have to sell. Radio is also very expensive, but not necessarily prohibitive. Unless you are very sure of your audience and advertising capabilities, it is probably best to avoid this form of media until your company is making lots of money and has a large advertising budget. But again, you can reach a lot of people with a radio ad. As with television, there are companies who will help you to create your ad.

Promote Yourself and Get Paid

There are a couple of other ways you can promote yourself while getting paid in the process. These are things you can do that, although they are not promotion *per se*, they will look great on your résumé.

Making Samples

Look at catalogs or product promotional advertisements for companies that sell products in your craft field. Check to see if they show pictures of craft items using their products. Chances are, they do. Someone has to make those samples—why not you?

Manufactures of sewing machines, jewelry findings, yarn, fabrics, mosaic craft tiles, paints, and so on, all want to show their products in the best light. This is done by having someone make up samples that they then use in their advertising and promotional materials. Most of the time, they hire the people to make these samples on a "piece-work basis."

A "piece-work basis" means that you get paid for the project, not hourly or on a salary. Usually, these companies will provide you with the supplies for the project and give you some general guidelines, but the actual design of the sample is left to you. This is a very creative outlet for your talents and can be a great source of income as well.

Working on a TV Show

There are two types of television shows that need people to sew or craft: one is the "how-to" show and the other is the home decorating show.

These shows need people to create all kinds of things. Depending upon the show, your skills and how you look, you may either be their "on-screen talent" or "off-screen worker." Don't be put off by being the person who works off-screen. They need a whole lot more people working off camera than they do on-camera.

Most of the decorating shows go from city to city doing make-overs to people's houses. They usually work on the make-over for one or two days and then move on. What the viewing public doesn't usually know is that in order to get the make-over done in the allotted time, they hire people from the local area to help.

Why Not You?

How do you get these kind of jobs? It isn't really that complicated. Find the address of a show you like. Think of the ways that they could use your talents. Send them a copy of your résumé and a letter explaining what you can do for them. Follow up with a phone call.

Promoting Through
the Internet

The Internet can be used to your advantage when it comes to promoting yourself. You won't necessarily make money immediately on the Internet. The payback will come much later. Using the Internet is another way to network with other people. The difference is that instead of networking with people in your local area face-to-face, these people will be from all over the country and possible even the world.

Chat Rooms

There are literally thousands of chat rooms and forums on the Internet. A chat room is a place where you communicate on-line by sending text messages to people in the same chat-room. The primary use of a chat room is to share information and enjoy the conversations of everyone in the room. Limit your search for chat rooms to topics that relate to what you sell. For example, if you sell wooden signs, look for chat rooms about wooden sign collecting or wood sign makers. You may want to join the first chat room to find out what people are looking for and the second to find others who do what you do.

Chat rooms will have a procedure for joining. You will need to pick a name to use while chatting and agree to any rules.

There are usually stringent rules for the members of a room to follow and there is generally a moderator to make sure the rules are followed. This keeps the room on topic. Don't bother with rooms that don't have rules and moderators. They will have people talking about anything they want and that won't be helpful for you.

Don't immediately start trying to sell your product to the other people in the room. This is considered rude and is often against the rules. Just get to know people. At some point someone will ask what you do. At that point you can state that you make your living creating your art.

Forums

Internet forums are also known as message boards, discussion boards, news groups, discussion forums, bulletin boards. The differ in several ways from chat rooms.

The most notable difference between a chat room an a forum is that a chat room is instant — you type on-line and when you hit your enter key, everyone in the room sees what you typed. In a forum, you "post" a message. How long before the posting is available for viewing for others depends upon the forum and how closely it is moderated. People look at the postings and then answer or comment if they choose.

Social Media

Facebook, Twitter, etc. are a huge part of our lives now. What they do for you is help people get to know you. Just like chat rooms and forums, they are not a place for selling directly. Post information if you wish, but don't spend more than a few hours a week on these endeavors. It takes time away from other areas that can be more productive. Its easy to spend way too much time on social media.

Etiquette

Whether you are in a chat room or a forum, the rules of etiquette apply. This just makes sense. You want people to view you in a good light. Some rules of etiquette include never typing in all upper case letters. On the Internet, this is equivalent to shouting. It goes without saying that manners are important.

HINTS ON ETIQUETTE AND THE USES OF SOCIETY

WITH A GLANCE AT BAD HABITS

There are short cut words on the Internet such as BRB (be right back) and others. Learn what these mean before using them. There are also smiley faces :-) and other "emoticons" that allow you to display emotion in your topics. You can find lists of these on the Internet so you can use them properly. Warning, over use of emoticons should be avoided since it appears juvenile.

As said earlier, never use chat rooms or forums to directly sell your product. If someone asks what you do, you can and should tell them, but don't try to sell them anything or you may find yourself kicked out of the group or people will disconnect from you in social media.

Labeling as Promotion

Your product label can be an effective promotional tool. Different kinds of products have different kinds of labels. They are a chance for you to tell the customer your story, tell them why your product is better than everyone else's. Labels also give you an opportunity to connect with your customer when you are not there.

Stick on Labels

If you have a product such as soap, candles, shampoos, something that is in a box, you can have a label that sticks on to the package. This label should have the

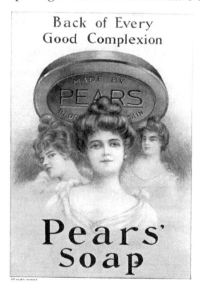

name of the product, a brief description of the product, the volume or weight if required (see Labeling Requirements on the next page), your logo, company name, city and web site, but not the price (see Adding Prices on the next page).

Hang Tags

Hang tags can be used for every product. If you sell rag dolls or quilts, unless you package them in boxes, a hang tag is the only way you can label them. A hang tag is usually made from card stock and hangs onto the product with string or ribbon. It is usually around 3 inches wide by 4 inches tall—although the size is up to you. If you sell jewelry, you may want smaller ones. A hang tag give you more space to talk about your product. The front should have your company logo, the product name and perhaps your company name and city. The back has the information about the product and your web site. Don't try to cram too much information on the back. People won't read it if it takes too long or the type is too small. Hit the highlights of your product and your company. Come up with a one to two paragraph narrative the makes your company and product sound fantastic.

Adding Prices

If you put a price on your label, it should be your retail price. When you sell this to your wholesale customers, this is known as the MSRP (Manufacturer's Suggested Retail Price). If you are selling to retail stores or wholesalers, whether or not you put your price on the label depends on your customers. Not everyone will sell your product at your suggested retail price. They may want to sell it for more. In that case, they won't want your price on the label or hang tag. You may need to have two sets of labels or hang tags—one with prices, and one without, and give your wholesale customers a choice.

Labeling Requirements

Some products, such as shampoo and clothing, have specific labeling requirements. For example, shampoo has to have the ingredients listed and the net volume of the product that is in the bottle. Clothing has to have the fiber content. Children's sleepwear has to be made from fire retardant fabric and it must say so on the label. Teddy bears and children's toys have to have age appropriate labels. For your product, you *must* find out the labeling requirements. Fortunately, you can do so on the Internet. The Fair Trade Commission and the Food and Drug Administration have web sites that explain in detail labeling requirements for products. Be sure you follow these to the letter.

P

passion
product
packaging
pricing
promotion

lacement

planning
profit

Placement

Placement is not only the way in which you get your product to market through shipping, it is also how you ultimately distribute your product directly to the consumer. This is also known as your "distribution channel."

Since you are small, your shipping methods will most likely be through postal service companies line UPS, Federal Express or the Post Office, so we won't cover shipping here.

In this chapter we will cover the following topics:

- ❖ What is Placement?
- ❖ Distribution Channel: Retail Stores
- ❖ Distribution Channel: Trade Shows
- ❖ Distribution Channel: Craft Malls
- ❖ Distribution Channel: The Internet

What is Placement?

Placement is about getting your product to the public through various distribution channels. Distribution channels are the logistics of getting the products to the customer. If you sell your items wholesale, then you may decide to place your products with wholesalers. They in turn sell them to their retailers. Placement is about making decisions as to how you get your product to the final consumer—this is your distribution channel. As always, there is selling involved. For example, in order to *place* your product with a wholesaler, you need to *sell* them on why they should carry your product line. Before you *place* your product into retail stores, you must *sell* the store buyer on the fact that they will make money carrying your product in their stores. In order to *place* your product in the hands of the final customer, you need to *sell* them on why they should purchase your product. In all of these three examples, there is *selling* involved.

These are not the only ways you can place your product. Although selling to wholesalers and retailers is effective, the following sections of this chapter describe these and various other distribution channels. You may decide to use one or many of them. Some may work early on in your business while others may work for you later on.

Distribution Channel: Retail Stores

Having your goods sold in retail stores nationwide is probably one of your dreams. While you may not be able to sell across the nation at first, selling at retail stores is not out of your reach.

Immediate Sale or Consignment

When you sell to retail stores, you will need to decide whether you want to have them purchase your goods immediately or purchase on consignment. You may end up doing both.

When you sell your goods immediately, your customer (the retailer) will place a purchase order with your company for the goods they want. You will fill that order and ship it to them. Their payment should be made in one of three ways: by check with the order, by "pro-forma" (which means they pay by check before the goods ship), or by credit card at time of order. As a small business, you probably can't afford to give credit terms and have the store pay invoices 30 days after the date of shipment.

Consignment, on the other hand, is where you place your goods at the retail-ers store. You give them an invoice for the goods. At the end of a time period that you agree upon with the store manager or owner, you will either get paid for the goods or receive them back. The consignment period is usually six months, but you can negotiate any time period that suits you and that the store owner will agree upon.

While the ideal situation for you would be to sell your goods immediately, sometimes it can be to your advantage to sell through consignment. The store owner may not be absolutely sure that your product will sell in their store. Telling them that you are willing to put your goods into their store on consignment will often get your foot in the door. Once they sell, you can ask for money up front for subsequent orders.

Local Gift Shops

There are probably more than a dozen gift shops in your local area; say within 25 miles or so, that would love to sell your product if they knew about it. So, make your appointment and see if you can get an order.

Local gift stores have an advantage for you because they are so close. You won't have to travel too far to meet with them. You can deliver your order yourself and save the shipping charges. You can tell your friends where you are selling your goods and they can go there to purchase your goods. You can even have your friends ask a store you would like to sell to if they carry your goods. When the store says "no,"—maybe *they* will call *you*. After all, they just had a request for your item.

A local gift shop is also a good choice when you are a beginner because they will generally only place a small order to start with. Since you will be making the goods yourself, you won't be over-whelmed filling the order. When you are ready, you can visit another store and get another order.

Don't forget to go the stores that previously ordered from you and ask if they would like to place a second order.

National Department Stores

National department stores will sometimes let you talk to their buyers. If so, you probably will have to work with them long distance, but in this day and age that's not as hard as it used to be.

Placement

You can email photos and brochures. You may need to send samples so they can see your work up-close. It is possible to sell to a national store such as Macy's, Neiman Marcus, and others directly through their buyers. They are always looking for products that are upscale and unique that appeal to their customers. Remember that although many of these stores go to the national gift shows to find new products from small manufacturers, they also will deal directly with you if you have a product they believe will sell in their stores.

Discount Stores

You've probably noticed by now that nowhere in this book is it said you can't do something. It is *your* business, you can do whatever *you* like. That's the great part of owning your own company. So having said that, you *can* sell to discount stores if you want to. It is probably harder to speak to the buyer. Some discount stores have their purchasing departments in other countries. Once you sell to them, you should be aware that you will have to *deeply* discount your goods—that's why they are called discount stores. You will make up for the discount by selling in volume. If you have the capability to fill the orders, you can probably afford to make less per unit because of the higher volume.

National Gift Shows

A national gift show is a place where you can show your product to potential buyers. Believe it or not, it isn't as hard as you might think to get into these shows. There are major shows each year in cities like Los Angeles, New York, Dallas and San Francisco. There are also smaller shows in many other cities. They all have web sites where you can request booth space. Here's the catch, *it costs money to rent a booth.*

If you feel your product is ready and you can fill large orders, then this will be money well spent. It's something you may want to think about after your business is up and running.

Read the section on trade shows in this chapter. It has information about renting booth space. The same rules apply when renting booth space at a gift show.

Distribution Channel: Trade Shows and Conventions

Think about selling what you make at a trade show or convention. These can be very profitable. After all, you have hundreds or even thousands of people coming to you instead of you having to find them.

There are literally thousands of trade shows and conventions selling booth space for you to rent. Some of them are fantastic, but others can be disastrous especially if almost no-one from the buying public shows up.

There is more to your costs for a show than the booth cost. Most booths don't include tables, chairs, power, etc. There will also be food costs. If you have to travel to the show there will be costs for transportation and hotel. All of this adds up. Yet, you need to make a profit. There are so many shows and you can only attend a couple per year so figure out the *total costs* carefully before you make your choice. You will be selling at your full retail price, which helps, so keep that in mind when making your calculations.

How do you choose?

Choosing the right trade show can be difficult. The promoters will always tell you how great *their* show is going to be. They sell booth space and need you as their customer. Here are some things to consider:

Juried or non-juried

A *juried* show means that there are judges who evaluate the work of the prospective artists and only offer booth space to the best artists for each of a type of goods. In theory, there will only be a limited num-ber of each product type at these kind of shows. A non-juried show on the other hand allows anyone who applies to have booth space based on a first-come, first-served basis.

A *non-juried* show usually will let anyone in who pays the fee. It doesn't necessarily mean that non-juried is a bad show; like all shows, it depends upon the promoter. For someone new to the business, it may be the only type of show you can attend at first because unlike many juried shows, non-juried shows do not have as many requirements.

How many years has the show been running?

While the number of years is not always a perfect indicator of the success you will have at a particular show, it is useful to know. However, if the show is new, how successful the show will be is only a guess for the first or second year. If a show is new, the price of the booth should be lower than longer running shows. You may have more negotiating room with a new promoter because they may not have enough vendors to fill their booths in the first couple of years. If a show is well established, you should be able to get more reliable figures for attendance.

What was last year's attendance?

Even if the show has been running successfully for 25 years, you will *still* want to evaluate last year's attendance. Why? Because sometimes show promoters start to think that because the show has been going for a long time that they don't need to advertise or promote it any longer. Or, perhaps the public is tired of the show. It could be that the promoters have started allowing foreign goods in. You can't fool the discriminating buyer with cheap reproductions of real art. The quality buyers won't show up if the show does not real have products from real artists.

How is the show promoted?

As was discussed earlier, promotion is extremely important. It is no less so for a trade show or convention. As a potential vendor, you want the highest attendance possible. The higher the attendance, the greater the chances for sales. Ask the promoter how they will advertise the show and how many times they will do so. For example, if they say they will run ads on the local radio channels, how may times per week will they run them. If they are placing ads in newspapers, how many ads and what is the frequency?

Now What?

Once you choose which show to attend, the real work begins. First you need to decide what you will take to display. Your decision will be based upon the demographics of the show and the way in which you will get there. If you have to fly to the venue, you need to only take enough product that will fit into your luggage or that you can ship to the venue ahead of time. If you can't take the actual products because of space limitations, take posters with color pictures of your products.

The Booth

If you have done your homework, you will know the demographics of the show: are they looking for quilts, jewelry, ceramics, home decor, wooden signs or general crafts? Next, you will want to consider how your display will look. I once went to a trade show, set up my booth, stood back and realized it looked awful! What I thought was going to be a lovely booth just looked like a jumbled mess. The cloth walls were white, not black as expected. The white product I had looked terrible against a white backdrop. The lesson to learn is pre-plan what you want your booth to look like, but them be prepared to change it if needed. Always stand back and look at your booth when you are done setting it up. It should be eye-catching and interesting. You want people to come in.

Selling

The most important part of the trade show experience is selling. Unfortunately this isn't as easy as raking in the money. Some people will come into your booth and look around. Others will walk by. Still others will leave as soon as you try to talk to them. Be friendly and try to engage your potential buyers in a conversation about your product. Try to come up with an opening line to hook them. If they are looking at your product, saying something like, "I make these from antique fabrics and laces," will get them interested. If they ask you the price, don't be afraid to tell them and then tell them that you take cash or check. Ask them what color they would like. Assume the sale. Do this in a nice way. If you are afraid to talk to the people, you could end up attending the whole show without making any sales. Selling requires that you actively engage with the customer. You can't just sit back in your booth and expect (or hope) that someone will buy.

Credit Cards

If you are working at trade shows, you will need to accept credit cards; without them you will lose sales. This is part of doing business. Fortunately, there are companies on the Internet like PayPal that will let you process credit cards without expensive setup fees or minimum monthly amounts. You may also want to talk to your bank about their fees, minimum balances, etc. That way you can compare prices. Even if the bank cost is too high right now, it may be a better deal once you have more sales.

Distribution Channel: Craft Malls

Another way to place your goods with the customer is at what is known as a craft mall. A craft mall is a store that has an individual space for each seller to display their goods. To the customer, it looks like a regular gift shop. The craft mall takes care of the selling transactions for you. They take the credit cards, checks and/or cash. You don't have to worry about the credit card fees or checks bouncing. All this happens while you aren't even there.

Generally, these stores will charge you rent each month. On top of that, they take a percentage of each sale, usually between 5 and 10 percent. You price your goods at whatever price you want, but remember to consider these additional costs when you set your price.

These stores usually require a 6 month or yearly contract. Before you decide to enter into an agreement with a craft mall consider the following:

What does the store look like?

Go to the store as a shopper. Watch the reactions of the other customers. Are they buying? Look around at the other merchandise. It is similar in quality to what you will be selling? Will your goods fit into this store? If the store is full of country kitsch and you sell Victorian style goods, it is probably not a good fit for you. If you sell candles and almost every other booth is also selling candles, you may want to go elsewhere. Your "gut" feel is very valuable here. Go with your instincts.

Are others successful here?

If you can, talk to the other vendors. Do their products sell well? Ask what the vendor turnover is like. If they won't tell you or don't know, visit the store a couple of times and see if the vendors are all the same or if new ones have been set up.

If there is a waiting list for space, then it is probably a good place to be. If half of the space is empty and there is a constant turnover, it is probably because there aren't enough customers. Take your time finding the right facility for you.

Remember that in a craft mall, your product *has to sell itself.* People will look at it and decide based on appearance if they want to buy it. Merchandising is critical in a craft mall. The customer has to be attracted to your booth. Then they have to look at the merchandise and finally they have to pick it up and buy it—all without you or anyone else telling them how great your products are. Hang tags (see page 94) are especially effective in craft malls.

Placement

Distribution Channel: The Internet

Today, it seems that everyone has an Internet site. In fact, it's almost a requirement of conducting business. Having a web site and setting up an Internet store yourself are two different things. Before you invest in time and money setting up an Internet store, you need find out what it will cost and how often you have to update your information.

Instead of having your own Internet store, there are web sites that allow you to be a part of theirs; rather like an Internet craft mall. You pay a monthly fee to upload pictures of your products and the company site makes the sales and collects the money from the customers. They then take a percentage of the sale and pay you the rest. You fulfil the order and pay the shipping.

If you want to have your own site, there are some Internet Service Providers that have programs that, for a fee, help you to build a shopping cart for your web site. Credit card providers like PayPal have tools for you to take payments on your web site. This is especially good if you have a single product to sell because a shopping cart isn't needed, just a link to the credit card site. There isn't space in this book for all the possibilities here so again you need to do some research.

You also need to decide if you are going to sell your products wholesale to stores, or directly to retail customers. If you sell wholesale, you will need to have the customer contact you before they are allowed to purchase from your site. You will need them to send you their resale information. You need to make sure the buyer is a real store. You don't want to sell at your wholesale price to end consumers. You don't even want them to see the wholesale prices. This means you will need some kind of login. Asking for wholesale information and requiring a login is not an unusual request on the Internet.

Whether you sell wholesale or retail, just putting a site on the Internet will *not* bring you many customers. You will need to promote your web site as earnestly as you promote your business.

Selling through eBay™

A book like this would not be complete without talking about eBay. If this book were written a just few years back, the phenomenon of eBay would not have been mentioned. Now anyone can sell just about anything on eBay and there are literally thousands of books on the subject. They will all tell you that you need to do your homework before you start to sell. You need to see what others selling similar products are charging. Remember, people buying on eBay are looking for bargains. This doesn't mean you have to lose your shirt. You can ask a reasonable price if you have something unique or special that others want.

eBay can also be a place where you can sell your out-of-date items. If you have products that you no longer want to sell, but still have extras in stock, this is a good place to get rid of them. Take the time to learn how to do it. The eBay web site has complete instructions and even videos for you to learn the ropes. They even have a free program that will help you set up your goods for auction.

Selling on Etsy

Etsy is a great place for beginners because it is very inexpensive to set up a shop and they don't have a monthly charge. The one drawback is that many of the sellers, because they are beginners, price their products too low. Your products may seem over-priced even though you have priced them correctly. Another drawback is that people tend to say they purchased a product "on Etsy" (or eBay for that matter) instead of from you when friends ask where they got something. You want them to say they got it from you, not Etsy. Also, in order to get sales on Etsy, you have to promote your Etsy site - you might as well promote your own web site instead.

P

passion
product
packaging
pricing
promotion
placement

lanning

profit

Planning

Perhaps planning should be called the "forgotten P." We can *not* accomplish very much without planning.

This chapter will cover the following topics:

- ❖ Planning for Your Future
- ❖ *Worksheet Five* - Before You Start
- ❖ *Worksheet Six* - The First Year
- ❖ *Worksheet Seven* - The Five Year Plan

Planning for Your Future

Setting up a new business takes a lot of planning. It is important for you to have a *written* plan. Small business owners often try to run their business "by the seat of their pants" instead of having a written plan to help guide them though the daily, weekly and even yearly activities.

There are three worksheets in this chapter. They have been designed to take you through the planning process step-by-step. Once you have completed them you will have a simple business plan for the immediate future, for your first year and for the next five-years for your company.

You need to complete *each* of these before you start your business. They will help you succeed and will also help you to clarify your company goals.

Worksheet Five is about your plans *prior to starting your business*. There are quite a few things you need to do before you start your company.

Worksheet Six will help you plan your *first year of business*. These are the things you do daily, weekly and monthly.

Worksheet Seven will help you to develop a *five-year plan for your business*. You may have never considered a five-year plan, but having one will help you clarify your long-term goals.

Of course, once you have these three plans, you can and should, update them as your business changes and grows.

Worksheet Five—Before You Start

Get a notebook and some notebook paper. Divide it into one section for each of the tasks listed below. If you prefer, you can use a computer word processing program to create the pages of your notebook.

1. List the names of the product(s) you are going to sell, one product per page. Under each name, list the following:

    A. All of the materials and their quantities that you need to create your product .
    B. Each step required to make the product. Be as detailed as you can.
    C. The type and quantity of packaging you will need.
    D. The vendor(s) from whom you will purchase your goods for making your product or packaging.
    E. Research the requirements for your product labels

2. Find and secure the services of an accountant or SCORE Advisor and work with them to set up your checking account, your financial record keeping methods, get your federal tax id, and so on. They will help you define and set up all the financial aspects of your business. Add the information they give you to your worksheet as additional tasks.

3. Use the Contact Sheet on page 116 for each vendor from whom you need to purchase goods to make or package your product.

4. List each trade show you would like to attend using the Contact Sheet. You can decide later which ones to actually attend.

5. Use the Contact Sheet for each store that you want to contact to make selling appointments. You can decide later which ones to call.

6. List at least 4 types of promotion you plan to do, such as mailing brochures, print advertising, trunk shows, etc.

    1. _____
    2. _____
    3. _____
    4. _____

7. If you plan to promote via print advertising, list the name of the publications using the Contact Sheet.

8. How many products do you have to sell to break even?

9. With the help of your accountant or SCORE advisor, create a annual budget for each of the following:

    A. Goods Needed to Produce Your Products $_____
    B. Stationary and Business Cards   _____
    C. Brochures, Flyers and Advertising   _____
    D. Telephone & Mail Service   _____
    E. Administrative Costs   _____
    F. Trade Shows   _____

    TOTAL $_____

Planning

Contact Sheet

Type of Contact

    A. Goods Vendor
    B. Trade Show Vendor
    C. Advertiser
    D. Store
    E. Other _____

Contact Name: _____

Contact Company Name: _____

Contact Position: _____

Address: _____

City: _____ State: _____ Zip Code: _____

Telephone: _____

Fax: _____

Cell: _____

Email: _____

Web site: _____

Comments:

Worksheet Six—The First Year

These are the tasks you may need to do during the first year. You may not need to do all of these. Also, as you go along, you will find additional things to add to your list. This list will get you started.

1. Take pictures of all your products.

2. Design and print stationary, business cards and company résumé.

3. Design and print brochure, flyers and/or catalogs.

4. Design print advertisements.

5. Contact advertising departments from your list for advertising requirements. Place ads in the ones that suit your business (and that you can afford).

6. Determine how much product you need to make your samples to show on your appointments, and to display and sell at your first trade show.

7. Order your goods from your vendors to make your products.

8. Create enough product to show at first appointment.

9. Contact trade shows from your list to find out registration requirements. Register for the ones that work with your schedule and budget.

10. Create enough product for first trade show.

11. Contact stores on your list for selling appointments.

12. Go to your appointments and/or trade shows.

13. Reorder and create more product for any sales made.

Worksheet Seven—The Five-Year Plan

Your five-year plan needs to be separate from the previous worksheets. These are goals you have for the long-term. You may not reach all these goals, or you may change them over the course of five years, but it is valuable to have them written down. These goals are like a roadmap to your future. If, in two or three years, your business changes, write a new set of goals for the next five years.

Answer the following questions about your business as you expect it to be over the next five years. These questions are a recap of what we have covered throughout this book. In order to define your business and its five year goals, you need to answer these questions again. This time though, answer these as if you were giving someone an overview of your company, nothing too specific, just general answers. You should revise your five year plan every year.

> "If we are true to our plan, our statures touch the skies."
>
> Emily Dickinson

1. What is your company goal or mission?

2. What do you want your income to be five years from now?

3. How will your product range and sales grow during the lifetime of the company?

4. Who are your major competitors and what steps are you taking to compete with them?

5. What sales return do you expect on your product promotion?

6. Will you have to employ help? If so, what type of employee and what performance (sales, number of trade shows, etc.) do you expect from them.?

P

passion
product
packaging
pricing
promotion
placement
planning

rofit

Profit

Profit is the main difference between being an amateur and a professional. You want to be a professional so you have to make a profit.

This chapter will cover the following topics:

- ❖ The Most Important "P"
- ❖ What if I Can't Keep Up with the Work?
- ❖ Raise Your Prices
- ❖ Streamline Your Processes
- ❖ The Importance of Profit
- ❖ Now What?

The Most Important "P"

Y ou've learned about the traditional "Four Ps." This book started with an extra "P"—*passion*, then added two other "Ps": one for *packaging* and the other for *planning*, and now is ending with the most important "P": *profit*.

Although profit is not part of Marketing's "Four Ps" (it is generally considered a part of pricing), it really should have top billing on its own.

Discussions throughout this book have focused on how to calculate the cost of your product so that you can price it in a way that will make you a profit. As you get better at manufacturing your product, you should make more profit. Don't be afraid to raise your prices. As you get busy, if you reach the maximum number of units you can make in a week, one of the best ways to deal with this is to raise your price. This will do two things: decrease your customer base and raise your profits.

What if I Can't Keep Up with the Work?

Raise Your Prices

If you can't hire more people to help you, raise your prices! Raising your price may cause you to lose some customers. If you raise it too much it could lose you all of them. Doesn't this sound scary? Raising your prices should decrease the number of customers who purchase from you and this can help reduce the number of sales. The higher price should compensate for this.

You may want to try out your new pricing on your prospects first before you raise them for your customer base. If the new pricing doesn't work, that means you were at your threshold; at the highest price the customer is willing to pay. After a while if no-one buys at the new price, you will have to lower it again.

Start out by raising your price by about 10 percent and see what happens. Some customers may stop purchasing from you or some potential customers may choose not to purchase from you, but others will. The goal here is to make *more* money from

Profit

fewer customers so you can decrease your work load. Those customers who do purchase from you will be paying you more for the same goods. This will allow you to make a higher profit. You will be working less and/or making more money.

Streamline Your Processes

Another way to increase your profit is to streamline your processes. First you can lower your cost. The longer you are in business, the more predictable your company is. You will start to see trends in your sales. You may find that you sell your product better in July than January. You will also be able to predict the number of units you will sell per year. This will allow you to start purchasing product in larger bulk from your wholesalers.

Knowing how many products you sell each year will also allow you to make more of your product in a shorter amount of time. You can complete each portion of your projects on several months worth of items using a assembly-line method. Perform the first step on all items, then complete the next, and so on. You will be able to create a lot more products this way rather than one item at a time. You can also work on another group of products while others are drying or otherwise waiting. Look at your processing steps and see how they can be streamlined to save time.

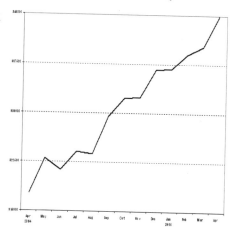

The Importance of Profit

Without profit, all the passion, product, packaging, pricing, promotion, placement and planning in the world doesn't matter. You *have* to make a profit or you are still only doing this for a hobby. Making a profit makes you an expert and a professional. Making a profit allows you to not only do what you love, but **to do it for a living.**

Now What?

You've read this book. Now what? Now is the time to put everything you have learned here into practice. This can be the intimidating part—but, no-one ever accomplished anything by wishing it would be so. Eleanor Roosevelt once said,

"No-one will admire you for what you *say* you are going to do."

How true. It 's easy to ***dream*** about what you want to do. Dreams are wonderful, but it is ***action*** that makes things happen. *Now* is the time for ***action***.

Go Make it Happen!

Turn *your* passion into profit.

Other Books by Kandi Christian

Turning Your Passion Into Profit
How to Make Money Teaching Your Sewing and Crafts
ISBN 978-0-9787127-5-4

Sewing for the Romantic Home
Volume One, Kitchens and Dining Rooms
ISBN 978-0-9787127-0-9